Marion &
Emilie Frances
Bauer

*From the Wild West to American
Musical Modernism*

To Janet.

Susan Pickett

Susan E. Pickett

ISBN: 978-1-4834-2291-6 (sc)
ISBN: 978-1-4834-2293-0 (hc)
ISBN: 978-1-4834-2292-3 (e)

Library of Congress Control Number: 2014921963

Lulu Publishing Services rev. date: 12/16/2014

CONTENTS

Dedication

To my husband
Robert Arnold Johnson

ACKNOWLEDGMENTS

I am particularly grateful to Robert Arnold Johnson, Jonas Myers, and Sarah Shewbert. I also wish to thank Michele Aichele, Donna Anderson, Katherine Axtell, Debra Bakland, George Boziwick, David Peter Coppen, Audrey Coulthurst, Amy Dodds, Joe Drazan, Sonja Gourley, Patrick Henry, Peggy Holloway, Jen Johnson, Marcus Lindbloom, Mary Anne O'Neil, Robin Rausch, Winifred Ringhoffer, Martha Furman Schleifer, William Shank, Ruth Liebes Shavel, Kile Smith, David Sprunger, Pat Stanley Matthews, Jonathan Sternberg, Fred Stoessel, Judith Tick, Elin Torvik, and Jackie Wood.

PREFACE

Emilie Frances and Marion Bauer were sisters who grew up in Walla Walla, Washington, in the latter nineteenth century. Each would become an American composer, writer, and music critic in New York City and would make an enduring contribution to her musical age, wherein modernism replaced romanticism. The sisters were prophetesses of and participants in modernism, Americanism, and the rise of professional music-making by women.

I have chosen to tell their stories through their own writings and correspondence whenever possible: they were excellent wordsmiths whose opinions resonate through time and who often deserve to be quoted at length rather than paraphrased.

I have provided considerable biographical detail, information about stylistic transformations, and the first comprehensive accounting of the music they composed. My hope is that future scholars will provide in-depth studies, particularly of Marion's music, which is woefully underrepresented in today's musical canon.

Their lives exemplify strength, courage, conviction, and a strong belief in womanhood. I hope I have done them justice.

CHAPTER 1

WILD WEST TO NEW YORK CITY

Wild West

Walla Walla (Many Waters[1]) is nestled in the southeast corner of Washington State. Creeks emanating in the nearby Blue Mountains crisscross the town. Mounds of thick, rich soil nurture vineyards and fields of wheat and onions. Main Street has an odd crook, mimicking the trail fashioned by Nez Perce Indians during a bygone era. Amid today's tranquility, remnants of Fort Walla Walla provide a poignant reminder of the bloody history of the region. The Fort was built by the Ninth Infantry in the mid–1850s, during the Northwest Indian Wars.[2] The town of Walla Walla sprouted simultaneously with the Fort.

Jacques Bauer was among the town's earliest residents. He was born into a Jewish family in Bischheim (Alsace), France, in 1834. At age twenty, he sailed from France to New York and shortly thereafter joined the Ninth Infantry.[3] The Infantry landed at Vancouver, Washington, and then fought in battles across the territory. Jacques served as an infantryman, then later as a member of the army band. He and several other members of the Ninth Infantry remained in Walla Walla after completing their military service. Although Jacques's children attributed his emigration to seeking adventure[4] and to his desire to learn English,[5] the prospect of a freer and better life for a Jew was surely a factor. Jacques, who adopted the nickname Joe, opened a tobacco store on Main Street.[6] Many of his earliest customers would have been transient gold prospectors who traveled up the Columbia River, gathered supplies in Walla Walla, and then headed to mines in Idaho and Montana. At the height of the Northwest gold rush in the early 1860s as many as 3,000 miners per month traversed this route.[7] Merchants in Walla Walla thrived as they catered to the needs of the miners. Mining tools, camping equipment, and other supplies dominated newspaper advertisements. Stores that sold liquor competed for the gold-digger dollar: "We have at all times large quantities of Liquors, put up in suitable packages for packing to the mines."[8] Thieves and vagabonds were initially unimpeded in Walla Walla. The absence of reliable law enforcement forced citizens to take the law into their own hands. Vigilantes rounded up "undesirables" and hanged them from a particular tree that was situated conveniently close to the cemetery. Horse thieves were shot.[9] Order was established in the town; bona fide law followed.

At a time of life when many men would have been contemplating marriage, Jacques was serving in the military and establishing his business. Even if he had wanted to marry, the tiny, barely-settled frontier town of Walla Walla was not a place where he could readily have met a young, unmarried Jewish woman. Fortunately, his brother, Robert, met the Heyman family in Buchsweiler (Bouxwiller), France.[10] One of the Heyman daughters was already living in Portland, Oregon. Another daughter, Julia, soon emigrated and moved in with her sister there.[11] Julia was an erudite young woman who spoke English, French, German, Italian, Spanish, and Hebrew. From France, Robert appears to have engineered Jacques and Julia's acquaintance. On 14 April 1864 they married at the Beth Israel Synagogue in Portland.[12] An anonymous reminiscence about Julia, written in 1913, shows that her adjustment to life in Walla Walla was difficult:

> In the early 1860s Mr. Bauer brought his bride to Walla Walla to make her home. She was a scholar and not accustomed to the pioneer ways of the time, when nearly every woman did her own housework. She was a wonderfully capable woman and could do almost

anything, but the care of the house wore on her nerves to such a degree that at the end of six months she was sick abed with a fever. During her convalescence she solved the problem of the household work. When sufficiently recovered she would organize classes in languages, and hire a cook. She succeeded beyond her expectations. So successful was she as a teacher that she never lacked for pupils, and Mrs. Bauer's classes in French, German, Spanish, and Italian, included many of the residents of the city today.[13]

When Julia was "sick abed" she was undoubtedly pregnant with their first child, Emilie Frances, who was born 5 March 1865. She may have been the first Jewish child born in the region.[14]

Downtown Walla Walla, ca. 1910. Jacques Bauer's
former store is the shorter building.[15]

As gold fever dwindled, agriculture flourished, transforming the landscape from natural grasses to wheat fields. Rising economic and social stability accompanied rapid population growth. In 1870 Walla Walla had 1,400 residents (Seattle had 1,100); by 1876 the population had more than doubled. The town prospered, though on several occasions from the 1860s through the 1880s large portions burned: straw embedded in muddy streets to make them more passable during winter became desiccated kindling in the hot summer; an errant match or lantern occasionally turned the roads into rivers of fire. Jacques's store burned to the ground twice. Two of Jacques's siblings emigrated around 1865–1870. His brother, Robert, worked as a clerk in Jacques's store,[16] and their sister, Leontine, married Jacob Jacobson.[17] Newspaper articles painted a picture of acceptance of the Bauers, Jacobsons, and other Jewish emigrants. Jewish merchants were an integral part of local commerce; closures of stores on Jewish holidays were respectfully announced in local newspapers, often with an explanation of their history and meaning. In contrast, Chinese emigrants, who helped build railroads in the region, often lived in isolation in tunnels and dugouts ("the underground"). Walla Walla had its own "Chinatown" about a block away from Jacques's store.

Jacques expanded his business to include general merchandise, musical instruments, sheet music, toys, clothing, and "fancy goods."[18] He wove himself into the social and political fabric of the town, running for city council[19] and county treasurer,[20] and joining the Independent Order of Oddfellows, Free and Accepted Masons, and Ancient Order of United Workmen.[21] It is speculative, but plausible, that Jacques and Julia were among town residents surrounding President Hayes in an 1880 photograph[22] taken in Walla Walla. A comparison of a picture of Julia to an unidentified woman in the presidential photograph is striking. The unidentified woman was standing next to a small man with dark hair; according to army pension records, Jacques was five feet four and had black hair.[23] Also, Julia is an obvious choice for the person who wrote the dinner menu, in French, provided at the meal for the President.

Culture and education were encouraged and valued by many residents in the budding town. The Whitman Seminary was established in 1859, which, in 1882, became Whitman College, a four-year liberal arts institution. During the 1880s, the town boasted Small's Opera House and Livery Stable, and Stahl's Opera House. Walla Wallans were entertained by troupes that performed the gamut of musical styles, from Gilbert and

Sullivan operettas to vaudeville. The military bands at Fort Walla Walla played frequently. Local bands and choral groups performed too. Jacques was a talented amateur musician who taught the rudiments of music to his children: "He had a beautiful tenor voice and had the ability to play any of the instruments in the military band. He entertained the family with an inexhaustible repertoire of operatic arias, frontier ballads, and French songs."[24]

The Bauers' first child, Emilie Frances, was born into an era when salon music was popular in middle class homes throughout America. This simple, melodious music, most often for piano or voice, was intended to be performed primarily by young ladies as parlor entertainment. Serious musical study was widely considered unladylike. Furthermore, a woman playing violin (which disfigured the face) was considered a ghastly spectacle, not to mention––heaven forbid––playing cello. Fortunately, during Emilie Frances's youth and early adulthood, the situation for women who desired to be professional musicians changed considerably. Emilie Frances was a serious musician, and when she needed advanced training, her parents sent her to San Francisco to study piano with Miguel Espinosa.[25] She turned fifteen years old during her studies there. Her age at the time and her gender lead one to suspect that she lived there with relatives who provided her with shelter, protection, and guidance.[26] When she returned to Walla Walla in 1881, at the age of sixteen, it was announced in a local newspaper, "Miss Emily Bauer, having returned from San Francisco, is now prepared to give instructions on the piano to a limited number of scholars."[27] This rather formal phrasing is not a surprise, coming from a highly educated young woman who was raised during the Victorian era. The Bauers' seventh and last child, Marion Eugénie, was born 15 August 1882. (Throughout her adult life, Marion fibbed about her year of birth, claiming 1887, but evidence proves otherwise.)[28] Thus, seventeen years separated Emilie Frances and Marion.

One month after giving birth to Marion, Julia began teaching languages at Whitman College. During the times that Julia was teaching, Emilie Frances helped tend to the needs of her siblings: Minnie/Minna (fifteen years old, who was disabled),[29] Cecil (twelve years old), Flora (ten years old), and Marion. (Two Bauer sons had died in childhood.) Marion was nestled in a basket on top of the piano in the Bauer home while Emilie Frances practiced and taught piano lessons.[30] Recollecting her youth, Marion provided insight into the family dynamics: "My mother was a linguist and a scholar who spent most of her life with her books. But it was from my father that I inherited my talent and love for music."[31] In this slightly acrid reminiscence about Julia, Marion did not give her credit for teaching her several languages, which was a decisive factor in one of Marion's early career opportunities. On the other hand, a caption of a photograph of Emilie Frances suggests the importance of her mother's influence: "The study of foreign languages is one of Miss [Emilie] Bauer's special delights, and her command of modern languages is of great value to her in her journalistic work."[32] It is unknown whether the other Bauer children learned multiple languages, although they were all fluent in French, which was the language spoken in the Bauer home.[33] Julia's teaching philosophy is evident in her advertisement in the 1889 Walla Walla City Directory:

School of Modern Languages
Mrs. J. H. Bauer
Teacher of German, French, Italian, Spanish,
Volapuk, and English to Foreigners.
These languages are taught by the means of progressive conversations.
PRACTICE BEFORE THEORY.
This reversed mode makes both theory and practise
most fascinating, and the study of languages
becomes a pleasant pastime instead of a task.[34]

Julia's advertisement shows that she had learned Volapük, which was a universal language developed in 1879. She taught Volapük in her home, formed the Walla Walla Volapük Club, and even surveyed the residents to discover their opinions about the new language.[35] (Julia did not have an aversion to teaching subjects more commonly associated with women, such as darning, point lace, and cross-stitch.)[36]

Whether the Bauer children participated in public school education or were home-schooled by Julia or Emilie Frances is uncertain. When Whitman

College opened its doors as a liberal arts institution, college preparatory studies were also offered, in which Cecil, the only surviving Bauer son, enrolled for four years. He subsequently attended at the collegiate level for two years.

Jacques and Emilie Frances participated in local musical events during the 1880s. On one occasion, Emilie Frances performed her own piano composition, "Murmurings from Venice."[37] Both she and Jacques received a complimentary review after their performance with the Oratorio Society: "The violin and piano numbers of Prof. Syminsky and Emilie Bauer gave especial satisfaction and brought a hearty encore from the audience. The vocal selection by Joe Bauer was given with good taste and in a pleasant quality of voice that delighted his hearers, who demanded his reappearance."[38] When another of Emilie Frances's piano pieces, "Moonlight on the Willamette," was published, the *Daily Journal* announced, "Miss Emilie Bauer is reported to have received lately from musical professors in Paris and Berlin, as well as from several noted ones in this country, very encouraging and flattering notices of her late compositions."[39] How professors in Europe knew her works is a mystery. A remote possibility is that Emilie Frances studied in Europe as well as San Francisco. However, the local newspapers eagerly printed news and gossip, and not even a hint of study in Europe has been uncovered elsewhere. That said, her early compositions reflect a good understanding of basic harmony and phrasing, but do not demonstrate a compelling creative impulse.

The year 1888 brought significant change for the Bauer family. First, Julia's association with Whitman College ended, but she continued teaching languages in her home. Second, Cecil entered law school in Portland, Oregon, and Emilie Frances moved there too.[40] The two did not share living quarters, and each established a professional milieu. For all its virtues, Walla Walla was still a relatively small and isolated town. By this time, Portland had a population around 20,000 and offered more musical opportunities for Emilie Frances. Two years after her relocation to Portland, the *Oregonian* published a complimentary review of her students' recital, in which they performed serious classical literature, including music by Beethoven, Kuhlau, Diabelli, Schubert, Mendelssohn, Brahms, and Chopin.[41]

Emilie Frances, now twenty-five years old, was visiting Walla Walla in 1890 when tragedy befell the Bauer family. The entire scene is recounted, with Victorian panache, in the *Walla Walla Statesman*:

Last Night's Fire

About 12 o'clock Thursday night a man standing in the back door of A. Byrd's saloon…noticed a bright blaze in one of the China houses…and immediately gave the alarm. A slight breeze was blowing and by the time water was thrown two buildings, one a Chinese saloon and the other an opium "joint," were enveloped in flames. On account of the narrow space in which to work the fire boys were nearly suffocated in their endeavors to do effective work, but they were successful, and saved the block…. The cause of the fire, as stated by the Chinamen, was the explosion of a lamp.[42]

Death of J. Bauer
The Victim of Apoplexy––A Family in Mourning

At no time in the history of Walla Walla has the populace received such a shock as was occasioned at an early hour this morning when it was learned that Jacques Bauer, one of our oldest and most respected citizens, was no more. Mr. Bauer was a man of good health and habits and the last person whom it would be supposed death would claim so suddenly as a victim. The particulars of his untimely death are brief. Himself and family had been visiting at the residence of Hon. Thos. Brents, and had just returned when the fire alarm sounded. He ran to his store, near the corner of Main and Third streets, in the immediate vicinity of which the fire was located. He was admitted by his brother, Robert, who sleeps in the rear portion of the building, but as he started toward the back entrance he exclaimed: "Brother, I am ill." Robert helped him to his room and immediately ran to the Palace, corner Main and Third streets and asked Hughy Taylor to telephone or send for a doctor, stating that his brother was dying in his room. Dr. Keylor was telephoned for, and Mr. Taylor and Robert Bauer hurried to the back room of the store, but during this time the deceased had arisen and gone to the watercloset in the rear of the building. Here he was found, and as Mr. Taylor endeavored to lift the dying man from his half-reclining position, the last breath was drawn and the spirit of Jacques Bauer departed from its temporary habitation. The body was removed to the store room and Dr. Keylor pronounced the sad news to the brother, who was completely prostrated with grief and wept like a child, and when the anxious wife and two daughters, Emilie and Flora, were made aware of their parent's death, a scene ensued which would have brought tears to the eyes of the most heartless.[43]

Funeral Ceremonies

The funeral of the late Jacques Bauer...was one of the largest ever witnessed in Eastern Washington, it being a testimonial of the esteem in which the deceased was held by hosts of friends in this and surrounding counties.... There were ninety-five carriages in the procession.

The ceremonies at the residence were impressive, conducted by Rev. Father Eagan, S. Simons and E. Jacobs, and the many old pioneer friends of the deceased found it impossible to keep back the silent tears as they witnessed the terrible grief of the wife and daughters to whom Joe Bauer had been so affectionate in life....

While the heartfelt sympathy of all citizens is extended to the sorrowing family, it is still gratifying to know that

Mr. Bauer was a good provider and leaves them beyond the pale of want.[44]

The ninety-five horse-drawn carriages in the funeral procession must have stretched nearly a half mile as they trudged toward Mountain View Cemetery. There, Jacques Bauer was laid to rest in the Jewish section, beside his two sons. Benjamin Rigberg, an historian of Northwest Jews, wrote a commentary on Jacques's funeral:

> The spectacle of two Jewish men and an Episcopal priest sharing in the ritual of burial for a Jew would have been highly unusual in an Eastern town. It is very likely that the rigors of frontier life and the need to be part of the community blurred the edges of religious separatism. Or, it may be that in a post-frontier settlement like Walla Walla, Judaism was accommodating itself to the reality of things. It is an illustration of how Jewish members in a community were accepted and then honored. At this time, they were not considered in any way different or separate. The Jewish members of the community, for their part, were obviously willing to participate in a ceremony that was not entirely Jewish.[45]

That said, Jacques may have been a religious skeptic. He was buried in the Jewish section of the local cemetery, which perhaps reflected the culture of Walla Walla at the time, rather than Jacques's personal beliefs. A letter written in 1883 by an acquaintance of Jacques's stated, "Mr. Bauer say he don't believe in the Bible but tells what other jews will do laughing at them although he will perhaps do as much as the others. How man has become even a jew don't believe that the old testament is of God. Bauer says that Moses wrote it, that he was a smart man, that it was good for them but that now they are smarter.... Miss B. [Emilie Frances] is free to take a Christian just so that he is a good man, says Mr. B."[46]

Portland, Oregon

Most of the Bauer assets were in their properties (the house and the store), worth about $12,500 at the time (the equivalent of about $315,000 in 2012).[47] During the probate period, Julia was strapped for cash, and the estate records show that she submitted a "petition for allowance," requesting seventy-five dollars per month (the equivalent of nearly two thousand dollars in 2012) until the estate was settled. She quickly decided not to sell either property, but rather to rent out both. Only two weeks after Jacques's death, and shortly after Marion's eighth birthday, the Bauers moved to Portland.[48] The entire family–Julia, Emilie Frances, Minnie, Cecil, Flora, and Marion–once again lived together. The relocation to Portland so soon after Jacques's death is startling. Perhaps Julia was seeking a larger population base to increase the number of students in her language classes, and thus increase her income. Or perhaps she never liked Walla Walla as well as she liked Portland.

Marion later recollected that Emilie Frances "became literally the father of the family, working with my mother to give the younger brother and sisters an education and every opportunity for cultural development. To her I owe the fact that I went into the serious study of music."[49] She also said Emilie Frances was "directly responsible for my musical education and has given me opportunities for advancement such as few young musicians get."[50] Marion was now old enough to begin piano lessons, and Emilie Frances was her teacher.[51] Their relationship appears to have been multifaceted: mother-daughter, teacher-pupil, and sister-sister. Later, as Marion entered adulthood, their connection transcended familial affection; they shared a passion for the arts, literature, languages, journalism, and, most especially, music.

Julia's home in Portland "became a cultural centre of the city and she was recognized as one of the pioneer educators of the Northwest."[52] Toward the end of the century she also taught for a few years at St. Helen's Hall, an Episcopal girls school, which boasted a rigorous academic curriculum. Marion attended high school at St. Helen's Hall and then Portland High School, which was a large coeducational institution.[53] The Bauers immersed themselves in the cultural offerings of Portland, including the Portland Symphony Orchestra, which gave its inaugural performance in 1896.[54] The soprano soloist was Rose Bloch, whom Cecil later married. Julia was a leader of the women's suffrage movement in Portland and she also learned and taught a new universal language, Esperanto, which overtook Volapük in popularity.

During the 1890s Emilie Frances was a music critic for the *Oregonian*, the largest newspaper in the region, and she was the Portland representative for *The Musical Courier*. The latter was a New York-based weekly magazine that circulated 1880–1961, whose representatives in several cities in the United States and Europe reviewed concerts and reported on local musical topics. The thirst of the American public for news and gossip about music was difficult to quench. *The Musical Courier* was one of several thriving magazines during the 1880s and 1890s; others included *Etude* (1883–1957) and *The Metronome* (1885–1961). Three more started around the turn of the century: *The Musician* (1896–1948), *Musical America* (1898–1964),[55] and *The Musical Leader* (1900–1967).[56] Emilie Frances's columns for *The Musical Courier* were infrequent––just a few each year in which she reported a handful of Portland events––which was in stark contrast to the myriad of events reported every week from New York and Boston. Her column from April 1895 was typical:

> Since my last writing we have not had many musical affairs, but what we have had have been good. We were accorded the pleasure of a recital by the venerable old musician Chevalier A. de Konski [Anton de Kontski; 1817-1899]. It is wonderful to hear the power and accuracy, to say nothing of the memory, of a man of his age. To talk with him, a pupil of Beethoven, a friend of Chopin, seemed like reaching back across the ages. [This was followed by reports on one chamber music recital, one piano recital, and one choral concert, plus the illness of a local singer.][57]

Did Emilie Frances yearn for a bustling musical center, like New York, where she would have so much more fodder for her music critic's pen? Apparently so.

New York Circa 1900

As cultural and educational organizations slowly emerged in the West, the metropolitan areas on the East coast boasted an abundance of symphony orchestras, opera companies, societies, publishers, philanthropists, music schools, and teachers. When Emilie Frances moved to New York in 1896, she was in the hub of music-making in America.

New York City had two major orchestras, the Philharmonic Society/ Orchestra (which formed in 1842) and the New York Symphony Society/ Orchestra (1878). The two orchestras competed for a while, then later joined forces. Others groups, such as the Philadelphia Orchestra (1900), also played regularly in New York. The Oratorio Society of New York formed in 1873, and the Metropolitan Opera opened in 1883. Chamber music grew under the leadership of the Flonzaley Quartet and the Kneisel Quartet, and the People's Symphony Concerts began in 1902, which were public chamber music recitals.[58] Several major American music-publishing houses thrived during the late nineteenth and early twentieth centuries, including Gustave Schirmer in New York, Theodore Presser in Philadelphia, and Oliver Ditson and Arthur P. Schmidt in Boston. Philanthropists such as Andrew Carnegie (1835–1919), Isabella Stewart Gardner (1840–1924), and Jeannette Meyer Thurber (1850–1946) generously supported American orchestras, opera companies, individual performers and composers, conservatories, colleges, publishers, and performance venues.

The desire for "American" compositions was being fueled in part by a Bohemian, Antonin Dvorak (1841–1904), with his presence in America in the 1890s, the popularity of his music, and his enthusiasm about the potential for an "American music." He was profoundly moved by the amalgamation of ethnicities, "Negro music," "Indian music," the vibrancy and beauty of the landscapes he saw, and the spirit of the American people. Everywhere around him, he saw the potential for homegrown American artistic inspiration. Several American composers became popular in this era and were received enthusiastically by the public. Particularly noteworthy were John Knowles Paine (1839–1906), Horatio Parker (1863–1919), George Chadwick (1854–1931), Edward MacDowell (1860–1908), Arthur Foote (1853–1937), and Amy Beach (1867–1944).

America was a lucrative performance venue for European musicians. Pyotr Tchaikovsky (1840–1893) was impressed when he learned that the German concert pianist Adele aus der Ohe (1864–1937) had earned $125,000 ($3,000,000 in 2012) during four years of concertizing in America during the 1880s. Tchaikovsky conducted four concerts for the inauguration of Carnegie Hall in 1891, for which he was paid $2,500 ($63,000 in 2012).[59] Many of the stars with the Metropolitan Opera, who were among the most highly paid musicians in America in that era, were born and trained in Europe. These artists were welcomed in the United States, but at the same time they engendered some resentment that European artists were given preference over homegrown singers.

Meanwhile, the prevailing idea that aspiring American composers and performers were essentially obligated to study in Europe to have proper credentials came under scrutiny and criticism. Paine, Parker, Chadwick, and MacDowell enjoyed prestigious appointments to the respective faculties of Harvard, Yale, the New England Conservatory, and Columbia. Ironically, these men, who had been trained in Germany, were now in a position to proclaim that their American institutions could provide the education necessary for a musician's art and craft. The debate lingered, but the robust seeds of an "American music" and an "American conservatory" were planted.

So too the landscape for aspiring women musicians changed in both Europe and America during the latter nineteenth century. Women virtuoso instrumentalists with indisputable talent and tremendously successful careers paved the path for future generations. Most notable were the pianists Clara Schumann (1819–1896), Adele aus der Ohe, Cécile Chaminade (1857–1944), and Teresa Carreño (1853–1917), and the violinists Maud Powell (1867–1920) and Camilla Urso (1842–1902).

Women also composed, just as they had always composed, but now the opportunities for education, recognition, and advancement were somewhat enhanced. The most obvious American example is the composer-pianist Amy Beach whose *Gaelic Symphony* and *Piano Concerto* were premiered by the Boston Symphony Orchestra in 1896 and 1899.

The number of women in America who became music teachers exploded from 1870–1910. In 1870 women accounted for 36 percent of people employed in music as a profession; by 1910 that had risen to 66 percent.[60] Within a few decades, women music teachers had changed their status from minority to majority. Women were involved in every other aspect of music-making as well, including chamber music and orchestral playing. Still, the largest and most prestigious professional-level ensembles were exclusively male. Women could participate professionally by playing with women exclusively. Professional mixed-gender ensembles were rare.[61] Community orchestras did provide opportunities for women.

Emilie Frances, New York Music Critic

Thus, when Emilie Frances moved to Brooklyn and taught piano there just before the turn of the century, she was no oddity. She continued to write for *The Musical Courier*, contributing one page per week about musical events in Brooklyn. After just less than two years, *The Musical Courier* sent her to San Francisco on a "special mission": the preparation of a "Patriotic Edition,"[62] "…[that] will give an exhaustive history of the past and present condition of the American Musician, composer, player, singer and conductor and teacher, and the prospects for the future of this large and influential class of our citizens."[63] Emilie Frances's familiarity with the West coast and her previous studies in San Francisco gave her an edge in recognizing the musical progress of the region. She reviewed concerts and reported more generally on musical life in the West. Her diagnosis of the situation emphasized the relative isolation of West coast artists: "Is San Francisco to be congratulated or to be pitied that its situation removes it from the close contact of a foreign or even Eastern atmosphere? Perhaps a little of both is due, with hearty congratulations that being, as it of necessity must be, dependent upon itself for its own musical atmosphere and influence upon the whole of this Coast."[64]

A month later she emphasized her disapproval of the perceived necessity of a European education for aspiring professional musicians: "In San Francisco, unfortunately, too much importance is put upon the 'European stamp of approval.' Here I want to be thoroughly understood. I have all respect for those who have studied hard in foreign lands, as well as those who have studied here, but this absolute necessity of a European label tacked on somewhere is what is going to upset the whole scheme in San Francisco, because it is such a hollow, empty one."[65] Emilie Frances's assignment in San Francisco was completed in February 1899. After a brief respite, it was announced that she would permanently be in charge of the Boston office of *The Musical Courier*.[66] Then, suddenly, at the end of March 1900, Emilie Frances joined the staff of *The Musical Leader*, and moved to Manhattan.

Emilie Frances Bauer, ca. 1901.[67]

The Musical Leader was a weekly magazine published by Charles and Florence French, who issued the first edition on 19 December 1900.[68] Florence French had been the Chicago correspondent for *The Musical Courier* for years, then directly competed against it with her own magazine.

The Musical Leader was headquartered in Chicago, but correspondents reported from numerous cities throughout the country and Europe, and several of those correspondents were women. Emilie Frances's weekly contributions to *The Musical Leader* were much more extensive than those to *The Musical Courier* had been. Of course, events in Manhattan gave her more on which to report, but beyond that, she seems to have had more freedom and space to express her personal opinions. She covered the Metropolitan Opera in detail as she reviewed performances, discussed what was about to be performed, and provided summaries of opera plots, information about the singers, and the names of new members of the orchestra. Every other major performing group enjoyed similar coverage. She reported on recitalists and their programs. She wrote about teachers who resided in New York City, announcing the names of their best pupils and which pieces they were performing. Personal information about artists was reported, such as who was getting married, who had a child, who was ill, who had died, who had an accident, who was sailing for Europe and on which ship they would sail, where they would perform, and so forth. Her essays were about topical issues, from her unwavering enthusiasm for Gustav Mahler as conductor of the New York Philharmonic, to supporting American music education, to complaining about concerts being held at conflicting times. She was an informed and concise journalist, who was very opinionated indeed, occasionally biting and sarcastic. Now, one century later, Emilie Frances's columns transport the reader back in time, tastes, and sensibilities. In her first (known) column, she wrote:

> Shall Music be Regarded as Amusement?
> People regard music as they do rare laces and rich velvets, in so much as they indulge if they can, and feel that they can dispense with the luxury if they must. They undertake the study, not as a matter of serious vital importance, but just because their neighbors do. Now, come to think of it, there is a close resemblance between lace and music, i. e., if either be cheap its vulgarity is glaring and unbearable to the cultured mind. Cheap music is the outcome of cheap teachers and cheap teachers live because the people who could support better do not know enough to do so.[69]

Each New York City music season lasted October through April. During those months, Emilie Frances reviewed an astonishing number of performances. She described the scene at the end of a season: "The musical 'lid' is down in New York, and the artists are flying out of the city in all directions."[70] She frequently left New York during the summer months, spending them in Europe or Portland or San Francisco. If during the summer she conducted interviews and attended concerts in Europe, those accounts were published. In addition to her work for *The Musical Leader*, and occasional essays in other publications such as *Etude* and *Harper's*, from 1902–1903 she was editor of the "Woman's Work in Music" page in *Etude* magazine. There she covered musical clubs and societies, pedagogy, philanthropy, education of women, women performers, and women composers. She was also a music critic for the *New York Evening Mail* from 1908–1914, and still wrote regularly for the *Oregonian*.

She formed tenacious alliances and loyalties and she seems to have been a quick and warm friend. Her education, professional position, and self-confidence empowered her to associate with luminaries of the New York artistic scene. A music student from Portland, Oregon (perhaps eighteen or nineteen years old) whom she took under her wing in New York City, described one of Emilie Frances's social gatherings, which likely took place between 1905–1908[71]: "I remember, at one of her 'afternoons in January' there were 28 world-famous musicians present. But with such honor guests as Garden, Caruso, Farrar, Mark Twain, Gabrilowitsch, Gadski, Sembich [Sembrich], etc., she did not overlook the little 'girl from home' who skimped and pinched to come to New York to 'study music.'"[72] What a guest list! Some of the greatest singers in the world: Mary Garden (1874–1967), Enrico Caruso (1873–1921), Geraldine Farrar (1882–1967), Johanna Gadski (1872–1932), and Marcella Sembrich (1858–1935). Mark Twain (1835–1910) requires no comment. Ossip Gabrilowitsch (1878–1936) was a Russian-born pianist, composer, and conductor who emigrated to America; he married Mark Twain's daughter, who was a singer.

Emilie Frances was subject to quick flares of temper, both in person and on the page. An amusing example is found in her letter to the editor in *The New York Times*:

Tuesday afternoon on a Broadway car the writer bethought herself that she had promised to stop at the butcher's on the way home. It also occurred to her that a transfer at Sixty-fifth Street would take her to the door on Columbus Avenue, and from there she would have but the one walk over. The conductor over-heard the conversation and the reason. I asked him for a transfer to receive his answer: "Why did you have to come 'way up here before asking for it?" I said I had only then remembered that it could be done that way. "Well, you get no transfer, that's all there is about it." I remonstrated. He leered and acted so brutally that men in the car ground their teeth in anger, while I was made the object of his jeers, and he gloated over the fact that walking would not hurt me. This took place on the car marked No. 504 and the conductor was No. 502.

Emilie Frances Bauer
New York, June 9, 1906[73]

One of Emilie Frances's friends offered further insight into her personality:

Though her early struggles to gain recognition were hard, she herself never grew so. She always held out a helping hand to "the other fellow" if he was square [honest]. If she found he was not, she was "through…." At deceit, hypocrisy or any double dealing her eyes would flash and she would "speak out" in denunciation.[74]

She would also "speak out in denunciation" in writing, exemplified by this essay in *Etude* which offers insight into changing social norms at the turn of the century:

Student-Life in New York
The first duty that somebody owes to the art of America is to establish a home of culture, refinement, and respectability in the large cities where students may board, live, and study with some degree of ease and safety. This idea of

sending young girls to New York to drift around into this house or that house in answer to an "ad." is nothing short of criminal on the part of parents, and at their door alone must be laid the blame of the consequences which are almost inevitable.

In the first place, unprotected young girls have no business in New York at all. Regarded from any side, that is the only thing I feel absolutely justified in saying. This old notion that if a girl cannot take care of herself at twenty she never can, is all nonsense. At twenty-five a girl is much more qualified to take care of herself than at twenty, and at thirty still more than at twenty-five. A woman of thirty is more willing to relinquish pleasures when it is better judgment to do so than a girl of twenty. This does not admit of a question, and it seems almost unnecessary to say that this qualification in itself is the first and the greatest.

Mothers bring up daughters in what they consider a pure atmosphere; of the evils that exist they keep them in ignorance, fearing that the very knowledge of things as they are would be a contamination; then they discover a little musical talent or a great deal of musical talent,—the amount makes no difference on the basis of morality,— and off they bundle them to New York. They do not know where they will live, they do not know with whom they will study, they do not know whom they will meet; they know absolutely nothing except that those daughters are in New York, no matter what else they think they know. That they are living in proper localities and surroundings they do not know; that they are studying under proper teachers they do not know; that they are associating with healthful companions they do not know. This does not mean that they are being deceived purposely; far from it. It means that the young girls do not know themselves, and when the awakening comes their first thought is: "Oh, I would not have mother know this for anything..."[75]

Another of her opinions––that a properly educated woman could potentially be a successful composer––certainly was not widely espoused at the time. One influential writer asserted that women who desired to be composers would never succeed because women were too emotional, too delicate, unable to endure discouragements, too dependent on intuition, and without the disposition for "theoretical application," therefore not teachable.[76] Sir Arthur Sullivan said, "It is a curious thing that, although so very many young women are exceptionally gifted, they only shine as executants. They do not seem to possess any real power, so far as composition is concerned. They can compose pieces much as the average man can write an intelligent letter, and just as you would not on that ground describe him as a literary man, the feminine facility in composition implies little more."[77] Emilie Frances took umbrage with those views:

> Women as Composers in the Future
>
> The subject of woman and her shortcomings on the creative side of music seems to be a source of never-failing delight to those who please to regard the subject from a psychic view or as a sex question. It is very strange, however, that, with all the speculations of the merry jesters, they have never approached anything like logic, and they never have anything to say except: "Well, they are not, and that is the end."
>
> There are a great many other fields where women have not held their own, and the direct cause has been that they were being taken care of by those who were their rightful protectors and the women that were thrown upon their own resources were comparatively very few, and these were hardly capable of meeting the situation in other ways than through the old avenues of teaching, dressmaking, millinery, etc. The quality of the work was not always

above reproach, but the fact that they were compelled to be breadwinners was enough to excuse all shortcomings.

The education of woman was, for the greater part, the most superficial thing imaginable. A little literature, a smattering of distorted French, still more distorted dashes of a few salon *morceaux*, and the young lady was ready for society. If she could play a little faster, through more limber joints, or a little louder, because of her physical development, than her neighbor, she, of course, was the artist of the neighborhood.

The danger did not end here, for when Dame Fortune turned coldly from the protector of the family, it fell to her lot to assist in providing a living, not only for herself, but for others, when she resorted as a matter of course to teaching music. Her music was bad enough, but that such should be propagated still further was, for the art, the most pernicious thing that could occur. As time went on there were those who studied more deeply, and they forced better work by creating a new standard; still it was superficial to a great degree, and is so yet, for that matter.

But women are forced into a different position in life to-day. From the cradle they are being prepared to battle with the world. The atmosphere surrounding their thoughts, their study, their development, their recreations is one which does not let them lose sight of the fact that they must work out their own salvations, and that their equipments must be superior to man's to come out even in the race.

Woman's mind has become more analytical. She is no longer satisfied to know that a piece of music is a concourse of sweet sounds, she must know why and how, and all about it. For this she must study theory, and then she has the tools with which to work. For talent, temperament, and every other attribute that can be remembered or that has been forgotten are valueless without theory and a solid foundation. The epoch of smattering is utterly and absolutely past, the day itself does not permit of it. Seriousness in all lines and in life itself precludes that flippancy in study which is the positive answer to the question "Why is woman weak on the creative side of music?"

As each day brings more women into the business world, into the world of deep thought, each day makes them more logical, more deliberate, gives them more control over their emotions, makes them more fit to bear the burdens of business lives. This same force that will make some of them financiers, scientists, inventors, littérateurs, will make of them composers, and not composers that will mince around on the outskirts of music satisfied to present here and there an over-sentimental melody which is a composite of everything that has ever been written, but those who will write music which is as deep as anything that has ever been called great.

One more matter cannot be overlooked, and that is that the child, born of the woman of to-day has in her favor the different atmosphere, the atmosphere which has raised women to a more intellectual, if not a happier, plane. So we may easily expect that the twentieth century will see the woman composer whose name shall be immortal.[78]

Why didn't Emilie Frances name even one preeminent woman composer, such as Hildegard of Bingen (1098–1179), Louise Farrenc (1804–1875), or Clara Schumann (1819–1896)?[79] It is likely that neither she nor any of her contemporaries knew much of their music. Even a highly educated and curious connoisseur did not have easy access to it.

Americanism, Women, and Music

During Emilie Frances's first decade of reporting on concerts in New York City, she established herself as a respected critic whose interests were broad and whose intelligence and wit were appreciated. Her pet peeves were the sluggishness of the American musical community in promoting its own and the sexism endured by women composers and performers of all countries.

Her fearless frankness was not the norm in music magazines. Magazine critics' reviews during this time have been described generally as "uncritical" and "nearly always, only words of praise."[80] Perhaps that was true for some, but that was not the case with Emilie Frances:

> Miss Bauer is particularly admired for her vigorous style, her fearless and just reviews, her clear exposition of current musical topics and her energetic campaign in the interests of pure art.[81]

> I have always been an enthusiastic admirer of Miss Bauer's critical and literary ability. In my opinion she is entitled to the honor of being one of the foremost women in musical literature today. Her style is vigorous and masculine; her ideas are original and scholarly; her ideals are pure and progressive; her essays are fascinating and instructive. Miss Bauer belongs to that class of writers whose works you await impatiently because you know there is something new to offer every time.[82]

Her review of the Dutch pianist, Edward Zeldenrust, is a case in point. First, *The New York Times* critic was fairly benign and vague in his criticism of a Zeldenrust performance:

> He is a pianist of distinct individuality, of temperament, and of large technical equipment. His judgment lacks perfect poise, and he does things which seem erratic. For example, he played Chopin's D flat valse faster than…

Rosenthal…. This is evidently what he was trying to do, but surely Chopin did not translate the antics of Georges Sand's dog into music to make a digital steeplechase. Mr. Zeldenrust did himself more credit by his…poetic treatment of the first two Chopin selections.[83]

Emilie Frances was considerably more critical and specific:

> The program opened with the Op. 53 Sonata of Beethoven, in which Zeldenrust proved distinctly that this enormous work was far beyond his mental grasp. His rubato treatment of the second movement was nothing short of laughable, and the third movement suffered from a total oblivion of the *una corda* demands, in other words, I do not remember that Zeldenrust used the left pedal at any time. He played the Schubert impromptu almost delightfully, as delightfully, in fact, as it can be given by one who has not a legato at his command.
>
> His Bach was admirably played…. Other numbers proved him erratic and changeable, without definiteness in anything, except to lower the record of Chopin's one-minute-George-Sand's-dog-waltz, which he did effectively, not, however, without leaving out about two measures in his haste.[84]

She also took the opportunity to campaign for American performers, using Zeldenrust as part of her ammunition:

> That Josef Hofmann played at the White House, set a standard hard to reach and only possible to surpass in two or three instances, and it is probable that America cannot claim five or six artists of that caliber––but it has one or two. That Zeldenrust played at the White House must open the door to at least a dozen American pianists, who are infinitely superior in every sense of the word. We do not ask that Americans be elevated into the

public eye because they are Americans. There could be nothing more menacing to the art; but we do ask that artists be not buried and deprived of honor because they are Americans.[85]

Concert managers and the public did often accord European performers what Emilie Frances called an automatic "stamp of approval," whereas American artists worked harder for recognition. American composers struggled as well, which was the grist for another biting Bauer essay:

The American composer has been well-nigh wiped off the musical map and there is no one in this season, the veins of which are overfilled to a point of bursting, who has the energy or the time to urge a plea. It is a pity, it is a shame that at this late day, there must be prayers and pleas, there must be begging and cringing and inducing and flattering for the purpose of securing one poor miserable little presentation without rehearsal and without interest in the works of our own people.[86]

One year later Emilie Frances had more hope for the prospects of American composers:

Arnold Volpe, conductor of the Volpe Symphony Orchestra, will present Edgar Stillman-Kelley's overture to "Macbeth" as the first feature of his plan to include American works at his concerts this winter.... And if these and others will only be steadfast in a serious endeavor, they will soon learn that the supply will equal the demand and that while some will be interesting others will not be, just the same as we enjoy some of the modern Germans, French and Italians and not others.[87]

While it is true that a few more American works were being performed by major ensembles, the contest between American and European composers, which was often paired with the contest between new and old, was just beginning. In contrast, the contest between male and female composers and performers was nearly as old as Western music itself. During the years following her 1901 essay "Women as Composers in the Future" Emilie Frances was more attentive to women composers and performers alike. For example, "The death of Augusta Holmes removes from France its most brilliant feminine composer, and now perhaps her works will come into the notice which by their merit they deserve.... The height reached by this talented woman makes a standard of high altitude that must be reached by other women who wish to shine as composers, for she had the force and the seriousness of a man with the delicacy and the grace of a woman."[88] How much of Augusta Holmes's (1847–1903) music Emilie Frances had heard is unclear. She obviously claimed knowledge of it and admired it, but only a few of Holmes's songs and none of her major orchestral works or operas had been presented in New York. Emilie Frances's attribution of "force" and "seriousness" to men and "grace" and "delicacy" to women is sexist in our current culture; she may be claiming that composers whose music blends both "male traits" and "female traits" is admirable. Yet, more than a century later, musicians and audiences alike have yet to objectively determine if these aural gender differences really exist. Emilie Frances seems to think they do, but are not mutually exclusive in the music of one gender as compared to another. Here is another example in her review of Ethel Smyth's (1858–1944) opera:

> That the Metropolitan stage should be given over to the work of a woman even for one hour is encouraging to say the least. But after one has seen the opera of Miss Ethel Smyth it is not difficult to realize that the play was put on because of its merit and not because it is the work of a woman, therefore a novelty in the way of interest.... Miss Smyth figures not only as the musical composer, but she is also her own librettist, and her book is a good one, containing much that is thoughtful and poetic. The music is incomparably better than anything that I have heard from Chaminade or from Mrs. Beach, who are the first women with whom she is naturally brought into comparison. Her thematic material is good, and

the orchestra is handled with virility and force quite remarkable in a woman.[89]

That Emilie Frances would belittle the music of Amy Beach and Cécile Chaminade in comparison to Smyth's is odd. *Der Wald* is a good work, but Beach's *Gaelic Symphony* and *Piano Concerto* and Chaminade's two piano trios are arguably as good. In her defense, Emilie Frances probably did not yet know these substantial works (she would later rave about Beach's symphony) and was very likely basing her judgment only on their salon songs and piano pieces, some of which would not compare favorably to Smyth's opera. Notice as well that she was surprised at the "virility and force" of Smyth's music. Emilie Frances was obviously comfortable with generalizing certain compositional traits as male or female, but not so with regard to performers:

> Now is the time for the fair sex to arise in horror at the flattering opinion which in Mr. [W. J.] Henderson's secret heart he holds of their art. It is true that Mr. Henderson has never made many women very happy by compliments, or at least not through the columns of the *Sun*, where his compliments would do the most good. But now he lets "the cat out of the bag" by stating in his criticism of Mme. Roger-Miclos [pianist], that "in power she reached a degree as large as might fairly be expected of a woman." Oyez! Oyez! Adele aus der Ohe, Fannie Bloomfield-Zeisler, Teresa Carreno, it is not expected of ye, but if ye have it not, beware![90]

In other words, Emilie Frances seems to expect the best female performers to directly compete with male performers in terms of physical power and virtuosity. She mentioned Adele aus der Ohe in the above criticism (who was noted earlier as the pianist at the inauguration of Carnegie Hall). Aus der Ohe relocated from Germany to New York during the time Emilie Frances lived there. It is unknown whether the two knew one another (although it is very likely, given Emilie Frances's large social circle), but Emilie Frances did review many of her numerous performances:

As her art grows more mature it takes on qualities of delicacy and of emotionality which were lacking in her earlier years, when her virtuosity was predominant. Now even the virtuosity has grown, but so superior are the other qualities that one forgets to marvel at her wonderful mechanism....

Miss Aus der Ohe presented two of her own compositions for piano and her new Sonata for Violin and Piano. The violin part was interpreted by David Mannes, who certainly deserved much credit for presenting the work as he did.... Miss Aus der Ohe was not sparing of the violinist by writing her Sonata in F sharp minor, but still this peculiar tonality produced a new effect in tone color. In the third movement, a beautiful adagio, Miss Aus der Ohe certainly reached a point of nobility in writing which no woman has surpassed, in fact it is doubtful if any woman has equalled it. It is unfair to bring the sex into the matter, as there has been little in the way of chamber music presented in years beside which this work may not take its place.[91]

Here Emilie Frances lauds aus der Ohe's pianistic maturation with attention to "delicacy" and also praises her technical prowess; this is more evidence that Emilie Frances was seeking a blend of "male and female traits" in great artistry. What is odd is her declaration that, compositionally speaking, aus der Ohe's sonata may not have been supassed in quality by another woman composer. It can easily be argued that Louise Farrenc's piano quintets, composed around 1840, are superior to aus der Ohe's sonata. But, again, even the greatest of the European women composers were unknown in America (and sometimes in their own countries).

Before Cécile Chaminade ever set foot on American soil her salon music was exceptionally popular throughout the country--so much so that numerous Cécile Chaminade Clubs formed. Little of her serious art music was known in America, and Chaminade did not remedy that during her first American performance, which Emilie Frances reviewed:

> The name of Chaminade is so familiar to the musical world that it seems strange to chronicle this as her first appearance in America, yet this is perhaps not strange in point of the fact that she never gave very much attention to the virtuoso's side of the art as her numerous number of compositions will attest. It was, therefore, an agreeable surprise to hear the grace and the charm with which she played her compositions, and since they are of the type known as salon pieces, they did not make very heavy demands upon her. Her technic is crisp and easy, and she has the grace which may be expected in one of her nationality.... Many of Mme. Chaminade's songs are of great beauty, yet few were sung...which have not been frequently upon the programs of local singers. It is almost needless to say that a very large audience was present, as the interest to see and to hear Mme. Chaminade is experienced by an unlimited number who have played and loved her compositions. Among these were many young girls and young women, who do not find their way to the concert room under ordinary circumstances, and there is no doubt that Mme. Chaminade will return to France with the conviction that she is known and well loved in America.[92]

Would Emilie Frances's mix of mild admiration with a tinge of scorn have been different if Chaminade had included at least one of her major chamber works on the program, one that demonstrated considerable virtuosity? Chaminade's tour of America lasted several weeks and at the end of it she performed again in New York. On her farewell concert she included one of her pianos trios and Emilie Frances remarked, "Mme. Chaminade again played a number of her piano pieces and...she played a very interesting and beautiful trio."[93] (Whether Chaminade performed her first or second piano trio is unknown, but in either case these very worthy chamber works have recently enjoyed a resurgence of interest.) Both of Chaminade's trios call for considerable virtuosity from the pianist; it is curious that Emilie Frances did not remark about this, given her previous comments.

The essays and reviews quoted here were selected specifically to spotlight Emilie Frances's thoughts about women composers, women performers, and Americanism at the advent of the twentieth century. She is attentive to the contemporary preeminent women composers and performers. We may guess, based on several of her comments, that she was uninformed about earlier women composers, including those now so conspicuous as Clara Schumann and Louise Farrenc. Emilie Frances committed the error that too many music historians and critics made then, and sometimes continue to make now: the presumption that if educated connoisseurs have not heard outstanding music by women composers, then it doesn't exist. Over the decades, Emilie Frances frequently lectured to her weekly audience that women composers and performers needed only talent, education, and opportunity to directly compete with male artists. That is true. Having her younger sister now aspire to become a composer would reinforce the vigor with which Emilie Frances would write about women composers in particular and American composers in general.

Emilie Frances Bauer, ca. 1903.[94]

Marion Moves to New York

As a teenager, Marion stated that she was torn among studying music, writing, teaching, and drawing.[95] Her high school years were not typical of a young musician: no record of serious piano study after Emilie Frances left Portland has been uncovered, nor have any youthful compositions. The "class statistics" page in her Portland High School year book indicated that singing was her "amusement," her aspiration was "to obtain a higher education," and that her "record in history, 2000 A. D." would show she was "a noted teacher of French."[96]

Marion Bauer is second from the front of this 1898 photograph of members of the St. Helen's Hall class, taken in front of the Bauer house in Portland.[97]

When Marion moved to New York City sometime between 1901 and 1903[98] she, in her own words, "followed the path of least resistance"[99] and immediately began piano and composition lessons with Henry Holden Huss (1862–1953).[100] Why was this the path of least resistance? Was she encouraged by Emilie Frances to pursue music? Had others recognized her talent? Were Emilie Frances's connections in New York opening doors for Marion otherwise shut to a young woman? We don't know, but we can guess that all were true. Around the time that Marion moved to New York, another Bauer sister, Flora, joined Marion and Emilie Frances there and the three shared an apartment.[101]

In Henry Holden Huss's studio piano recitals, Marion performed pieces by Huss himself. Emilie Frances reviewed one of these: "It was the privilege of Miss Marion Bauer to play two Intermezzi by Mr. Huss. In these she revealed beautiful tonal qualities and very decided musical temperament, with a keen perception for the inner beauties of the compositions with which she showed a keen sympathy."[102] Note, however, that the technical level of the pieces Marion played is quite modest—certainly not the caliber of works played by an aspiring and accomplished performer—but many composers develop their piano skills largely as a tool to assist composing.

In 1904, two of Marion's solo piano compositions were published. "Arabesque" and "Elegie" are simple and unsophisticated, and neither of the works adumbrates Marion's later modernism. "Elegie," for example, has a melody in the right hand and chords in the left hand throughout the entire composition. She had not yet thoroughly grasped basic harmonic principles, so her chord choices are occasionally odd, and her modulations (changes from one key to the next) are awkward. That said, she was only twenty-two when they were published, and she had just recently commenced her formal theory and composition studies. Both pieces do hint at her lifelong proclivity for a strong melodic line and her attention to an evocative mood. She received small royalties for her two pieces and she also had a few piano students, but at this stage of her life she does not appear to have been self-sustaining. Presumably, Emilie Frances provided room and board.

Marion's horizons were further broadened by a fortuitous encounter with Raoul Pugno (1852–1914), an internationally renowned French pianist. Pugno commenced an extensive concert tour in America in 1905, using New York City as his home base. Because his tour lasted several months, his wife and child traveled with him. None of the Pugnos were fluent in English, so Marion taught them the language. In exchange, Pugno invited Marion to live at his villa in Gargenville (near Paris), study piano with him, and experience French culture. Marion accepted the invitation, which was the first of several European sojourns the two sisters would make, independently of one another, during the next few years.

---

1   "Welcome to the City of Walla Walla," *City of Walla Walla*, accessed 8 August 2014, www.ci.walla-walla.us/visitors/history. The name is a Nez Perce Native American word that means "many waters" or "running waters."

2   Fort Walla Walla had several locations, the last of which was where the Jonathan Wainwright Memorial VA Hospital is now situated.

3   New York, Passenger Lists of Vessels Arriving at New York, New York, 1820–1897, micropublication M237, microfilm roll 142, list number 864, http://ancestry.com (accessed 19 May 2006); Pension Records, Indian War Veterans and Widows, Affidavit by Julia H. Bauer, 7 July 1902, National Archives.

4   Madeleine Goss, *Modern Music-Makers* (Westport, CT: Greenwood Press, 1952), 130. The way the section about Marion is written implies that Goss relied on extensive input by Marion.

5   David Ewen, *Composers of Today*, 2nd ed. (New York: H.W. Wilson Company, 1936), 15. The section about Marion is largely an autobiographical sketch written by Marion.

6   His store was near the current northeast corner of Main Street and Third Avenue.

7   Robert Bennett, *Walla Walla: Portrait of a Western Town, 1804–1899* (Walla Walla, WA: Pioneer Press Books, 1980–1982), 62.

8   *Washington Statesman*, advertisement of Gumiston, Wilson & Co., 6 Sep 1862, 3.

9   Bennett, 67.

10 Pension Records, Indian War Veterans and Widows, Affidavit by Robert E. Bauer for claim of Julia Bauer, widow of Jacques Bauer, 16 July 1903, National Archives.

11 "Noted Linguist Dead at Age of 70 Years." Newspaper clipping of unknown origin. Nellie Day scrapbook. (Walla Walla, WA: Whitman College archives, Bauer folder), [July 1913]; Registres de l'état civil, 1793–1882 Bouxwiller (Bas-Rhin), officier de l'état civil (official birth records for Bouxwiller, France) http://www.familysearch.org. Julia/Julie was the daughter of Jacques Heymann and Rachel Klemann. Her birth name was Julie, which was anglicized to Julia after her arrival in America. Her last name is most often spelled "Heyman" in American legal documents and Heymann or Heimann in European records. American records indicate Julia's year of birth as 1843, which is indicated on her gravestone, but the French and German records state 1842. Julia's father may have married three times. If so, Julia was born to his third wife; the sister in Portland may have been Rosalie Heyman Cahn.

12 *The Daily Oregonian*, "Married," 15 Apr 1864, 2.

13 "Fragments of Early History," *Up to the Times Magazine*, Feb 1913, 4913–4914.

14 Benjamin Rigberg, *Walla Walla: Judaism in a Rural Setting* (Los Angeles: Western States Jewish History Association, 2001), 36.

15 Main Street Parade, 1910, from *Historic Walla Walla Valley, Washington*, Vol. 1, DVD, ed. Joe Drazan, (2007; Walla Walla, WA). By permission of Joe Drazan.

16 *Walla Walla Daily Union*, "R. E. Bauer Dies When Leg is Amputated," 5 Oct 1906, 1.

17 Rigberg, 46. Indisputable evidence that Leontine was Jacques's sister has not been found, but the author is convinced by the overwhelming circumstantial evidence.

18 Jacques's *Walla Walla Statesman* advertisements throughout the 1870s and 1880s refer to "fancy goods" without defining what that means.

19 *Walla Walla Statesman*, "Citizens' Ticket," 23 Mar 1866, 1.

20 *Walla Walla Statesman*, [announcement], 23 Mar 1869, 3.

21 *Walla Walla Daily Statesman*, "Death of J. Bauer," 1 Aug 1890, 3.

22 Bennett, 105. Unfortunately, the condition of the photograph renders it not suitable for reproduction.

23 Pension Records, Indian War Veterans and Widows, Affidavit by Julia H. Bauer, 7 July 1902, National Archives. Personal information about Jacques was provided in a form that Julia filled out to receive her pension.

24 David Ewen, *American Composers Today* (New York: H. W. Wilson & Co., 1949), 20. Marion's recollection.

25 Espinosa was trained at the Paris Conservatory. Sometimes Espinosa's name is alternatively spelled Espinoza. Some sources have claimed that Emilie Frances studied at the Paris Conservatory, for which no evidence has been found. Also, an announcement in the *Walla Walla Union* "Personal" column on 6 Aug 1881, stated that Emilie Frances was an "accomplished performer and a singer of rare ability." No other evidence of singing ability has been uncovered.

26 Julia's probable sister, Rosalie Heyman Cahn had moved from Portland to San Francisco by 1880. Her half-sister, Emilie Heyman (alternatively spelled Heimann) Willard emigrated from France to San Francisco in 1884.

27 *Walla Walla Morning Journal*, "Local Laconics," 18 Aug 1881, 3.

28 *Walla Walla Morning Daily Union*, "Born," 16 Aug 1882, 2. "Born. In this city, Aug. 15, to the wife of Joe Bauer, a daughter." 1882 as her birth year is confirmed in the U. S. Bureau of the Census, population census of 1900 (Washington, DC: U. S. Government Printing Office, 1900).

29 *Oregonian*, "Miss Minnie Bauer Dies," 27 Aug 1920, 6.

30 Goss, 129.

31 Ewen, *Composers of Today*, 15.

32 Emilie Frances Bauer, "The City or the Country," in *Musical Essays in Art, Culture, Education,* selected and reprinted from *The Etude,* 1892–1902 (Philadelphia: Theodore Presser, 1902), 237. This information is from the caption of a photograph of her, presumably provided by Emilie Frances herself.

33 "Many Artists Singing Young American Composer's songs," *ML* 29/21 (27 May 1915), 643.

34 Walla Walla City Directory, 1889, Vol. 1 (Walla Walla, WA: V. Amp. Smith, 1889), 8.

35 *Walla Walla Statesman,* "Local Notes," 29 Aug 1888, 3.

36 Nancy Wilson Ross, *Westward the Women* (San Francisco: North Point Press, 1985), 17.

37 *Walla Walla Daily Journal,* "Presbyterian Church Concert," 22 Dec 1884, 3.

38 *Walla Walla Daily Journal,* "Oratorio Society Concert," 20 Jan 1885, 3.

39 *Walla Walla Daily Journal,* "People," 19 Mar 1885, 3.

40 *Walla Walla Statesman,* "Local Notes," 19 Sep 1888, 3. An announcement stated that as of Sep 1888 Emilie Frances had a "fine class" of students in Portland.

41 *Oregonian,* "Miss Bauer's Musical Recital," 16 Mar 1890, 9.

42 *Walla Walla Daily Statesman,* "Last Night's Fire," 1 Aug 1890, 3.

43 *Walla Walla Daily Statesman,* "Death of J. Bauer," 1 Aug 1890, 3.

44 *Walla Walla Daily Statesman,* "Funeral Ceremonies," 4 Aug 1890, 3.

45 Rigberg, 40–41.

46 Berney-Rochat Family Papers, correspondence from Eva Thonney to Annie [Berney], 10 October 1883, HTM_WCMss61, Penrose Library Archives, Whitman College.

47 All conversion rates in this book are from the online source www.westegg.com/inflation/.

48 *Walla Walla Statesman,* "Of Local Interest," 16 Aug 1890, 3.

49 Ewen, *Composers of Today,* 15.

50 Marion Bauer to Arthur P. Schmidt, 20 Jan 1915, A. P. Schmidt Co. Archives, business papers/correspondence/box 7, Library of Congress, Washington, DC.

51 Reliable sources about Marion's childhood do not specify when she began piano lessons with Emilie Frances. However, Marion was 6 years old when her sister moved to Portland, so bona fide piano lessons most likely began when Marion, now 8 years old, joined her sister in Portland.

52 Ewen, *Composers of Today,* 15.

53 Deborah Cohen, "Marion Bauer: Critical Reception of Her Historical Publications" (Ph.D. Thesis, U. C. L. A., 1997), 81–103. Marion also undertook post–secondary education at both schools; Portland High School was later renamed Lincoln High School.

54 Portland Symphony Orchestra, concert program, 30 Oct 1896, Portland, OR.

55 It continued as a section of *High Fidelity,* then other titles.

56 Most of these magazines catered to different audiences. *The Musical Courier* and *The Musical Leader* were the most similar and the most competitive for the same audience. *Etude* had several similar titles from 1883–1957.

57 Emilie Frances Bauer, "Portland," *MC* 30/16 (10 Apr 1895), 30.

58 Irving Kolodin, Francis D. Perkins, Susan Thiemann Sommer, Zdravko Blazekovic, "New York," *Grove Music Online*, ed. L. Macy, http://www.grovemusic.com (accessed 4 Nov 2006).

59 *The Diaries of Tchaikovsky*, trans. Wladimir Lakond (New York: W. W. Norton & Co, 1945), 310. Aus der Ohe played a Tchaikovsky piano concerto at the inaugural concert as Tchaikovsky conducted. She died a pauper in Berlin in 1937.

60 Jane Bowers and Judith Tick, *Women Making Music: The Western Art Tradition, 1150–1950* (Urbana: University of Illinois Press, 1986), 327. These numbers include private music teachers.

61 With regard to orchestral positions, equality came painfully slowly, and is not yet achieved in certain European orchestras.

62 "San Francisco," *MC* 36/14 (6 Apr 1898), 16.

63 "A Patriotic Edition," *MC* 36/14 (6 Apr 1898), 20. The "Patriotic Edition" was issued 4 July 1898 and was 169 pages long. A lengthy "National Edition" was issued 7 Dec 1898.

64 Emilie Frances Bauer, "San Francisco," *MC* 36/17 (27 Apr 1898), 15.

65 Emilie Frances Bauer, "San Francisco," *MC* 36/21 (25 May 1898), 28.

66 "Boston," *MC* 38/15 (12 Apr 1899), 26–27.

67 Theodore Presser, *Musical Essays in Art, Culture, Education* (Philadelphia: T. Presser, 1901), 237.

68 The magazine bought another publication in 1903, *The Concert Goer*, at which point the magazine became *The Musical Leader and Concert Goer*. In 1910 the title returned to *The Musical Leader*. During the Great Depression the magazine became biweekly during the music season and monthly otherwise, then during later years, monthly. An alternate spelling of their name is Ffrench.

69 Emilie Frances Bauer, "Shall Music be Regarded as Amusement?," *ML* 2/12 (19 Sep 1901), 5.

70 Emilie Frances Bauer, "Music in New York," *ML* 25/17 (24 Apr 1913), 567.

71 These dates for the gathering were construed by correlating when certain guests were known to be performing in New York, thus were available for a social gathering, coupled with Mark Twain's residence in America and his year of death.

72 Genevieve Thompson Smith, "Tribute to Emilie F. Bauer. Aided Struggling Artists," *Oregon Daily Journal*, 11 Mar 1926, 10.

73 Emilie Frances Bauer, letter to the editor, *NYT*, 11 June 1906, 6.

74 Smith, 10.

[75] Emilie Frances Bauer, "Student-Life in New York," *Etude* 20/6 (June 1902), 216. The ellipsis at the conclusion is original.

[76] George P. Upton, *Woman in Music* (Chicago: A. C. McClurg & Co., 1892), 19–30

[77] "Women as Composers," *ML* 1/3 (2 Jan 1901), 3.

[78] Emilie Frances Bauer, "Women as Composers in the Future," *Etude* 19/9 (Sep 1901), 321.

[79] Over 2000 pre–twentieth century women composers have been documented. Some of them clearly deserve immortality.

[80] Charles Lindahl, compiler and reviewer, "Music Periodicals in U.S. Research Libraries in 1931: A Retrospective Survey. Part III: The United States," in *Notes*, 2nd Ser., 38/2 (Dec 1981): 322.

[81] "Emilie Frances Bauer," *MLCG* 6/15 (8 Oct 1903), 13. *The Musical Leader and Concert Goer* reprinted this opinion from *The Bulletin* of San Francisco, 1903, without the author or specific date of the source.

[82] "Emilie Frances Bauer," *MLCG* 6/15 (8 Oct 1903), 13. *The Musical Leader and Concert Goer* reprinted this opinion from *The Musical* Review, 1903, without the author or specific date of the source.

[83] *NYT*, "Mr. Zeldenrust's Piano Recital," 20 Jan 1902, 7. The critic is not specified, but is likely Richard Aldrich.

[84] Emilie Frances Bauer, "Zeldenrust in Recital," *ML* 3/5 (30 Jan 1902), 10–11.

[85] Emilie Frances Bauer, "New York," *ML* 3/5 (30 Jan 1902), 10.

[86] Emilie Frances Bauer, "Nothing Accomplished for Americans," *MLCG* 18/27 (30 Dec 1909), 10.

[87] Emilie Frances Bauer, "A Tireless Fight for the American Composer," *ML* 20/18 (3 Nov 1910), 12.

[88] Emilie Frances Bauer, "New York," *ML* 5/6 (5 Feb 1903), 5.

[89] Emilie Frances Bauer, "'Der Wald'—A Woman's Opera," *MLCG* 5/13 (26 Mar 1903), 3.

[90] Emilie Frances Bauer, "New York," *ML* 5/7 (12 Feb 1903), 3.

[91] Emilie Frances Bauer, "Adele Aus der Ohe's Recital," *MLCG* 9/3 (19 Jan 1905), 5–6. Aus der Ohe's *Sonata for Violin and Piano* is indeed an excellent composition that, like most works by women composers, has not yet returned to the repertoire today and deserves another chance.

[92] Emilie Frances Bauer, "Chaminade's American Debut," *MLCG* 16/18 (29 Oct 1908), 8.

[93] Emilie Frances Bauer, "The Chaminade Farewell," *MLCG* 16/26 (24 Dec 1908), 9.

[94] *ML* 6/15 (8 Oct 1903), 13.

[95] Ewen, *Composers of Today*, 15.

[96] *The Cardinal* 3/10 (June 1900), 37.

97 The Oregon Historical Society, negative number bb001893. Permission to publish granted. The Bauers lived at 475 Main Street, Portland, OR.

98 Emilie Frances Bauer, "Some Huss Pupils," *MLCG* 7/18 (5 May 1904), 5. The first time Marion is mentioned as living in New York is in the 5 May 1904 *Musical Leader and Concert Goer* when she played in a Henry Holden Huss studio recital. This implies she had studied with Huss for at least one season. Given that two of her compositions were published in 1904 (probably with Huss's approval), it is most likely she had studied with him for two or three years by that time.

99 Ewen, *Composers of Today*, 15.

100 Goss, *Modern Music-Makers*, 130. Huss dedicated his 1944 composition "On to Victory" (a piano work written during World War II), "To my dear friend and pupil, Marion."

101 Their address was 240 West 97th. Exactly when Flora moved there is unknown. Marion had definitely moved to New York City as of 1904.

102 Emilie Frances Bauer, "Some Huss Pupils," *MLCG* 7/18 (5 May 1904), 5.

CHAPTER 2

EUROPEAN ADVENTURES

Marion in France

Marion spent the summer of 1906 at Raoul Pugno's villa, and then stayed in Paris during the fall and winter.[1] Marion recalled, "My mother was right when she said later that no 'castles in Spain' could have surpassed the glorious reality of that first visit to Europe. I was a member of the Pugno household and was treated as a daughter. I had a charming little room overlooking the gardens and the fountain.... I had my own piano and spent my mornings, after a half-hour walk through the beautiful estate, in practice."[2]

For the first time, Marion was exposed to the music of the newly famous Claude Debussy (1862–1918). Debussy was the father of musical impressionism, which followed closely on the heels of impressionism in the visual arts. He had composed *Prélude à l'après-midi d'un faune* in 1894 in which his "orchestral water colors" were fully mature and which became an historic hallmark of his style. During the time Marion was in Paris, Debussy was working on pieces such as *La Mer* and *Images*. His unique sound was, in part, the result of breaking compositional edicts in practice for hundreds of years. His novel approaches to harmony, melody, orchestration, dynamics, rhythm, and meter were all intensely scrutinized and often harshly criticized by Europeans and Americans alike. The term

"Debussyism" had just come into vogue, uttered by some as a compliment, and by others as an insult.

Maurice Ravel (1875–1937) was also active in Paris, but was initially overshadowed by Debussy. Camille Saint-Saëns (1835–1921) represented the "old guard." Gabriel Fauré (1845–1924) was a bridge between the two. When Marion arrived in Paris, Fauré recently had been appointed Director of the Paris Conservatory, one of the leading music conservatories in the world. Marion's connection to Pugno (who was a friend of Debussy), and her proximity to Paris suggest that she became acquainted with these luminaries of the French musical community. (She owned an autographed photograph of Debussy, but how she acquired it is unknown.)[3]

Pugno's villa was a popular gathering place for Parisian musicians, artists, and writers.[4] Among his frequent guests were Nadia and Lili Boulanger. Nadia (1887–1979), whose pedagogical and analytical brilliance were apparent even in her youth, became a legendary composition and analysis teacher. During her seventy-five-year career Nadia taught over six-hundred Americans, from Aaron Copland to Philip Glass, plus students from throughout the world. Her younger sister, Lili (1893–1918), who was a teenage composer-prodigy, died tragically at the age of twenty-four. When Marion met Nadia at Pugno's villa, Nadia was nineteen years old and Marion was twenty-four. Marion may have started lying about her birth year at this time as a reaction to Nadia, and maybe Lili too. It is fair to say that while Marion was talented, she was not prodigious. Moreover, students at the Paris Conservatory had the advantage of much more extensive and intensive training, at a considerably earlier age, than Marion would have enjoyed. Nadia reportedly proposed that if Marion would teach her English she would teach Marion harmony. The pupils in Marion's English class were Nadia and Lili Boulanger and Renée Pugno (Raoul's daughter).[5] Marion was Nadia's first known American student. Spending several months with two incredibly talented and ambitious young women must have been both exhilarating and intimidating for Marion. From Paris, she wrote a letter to *The Musical Leader* describing one of Nadia Boulanger's concerts and her own increasing understanding of impressionism:

On January 6 Mlle. Nadia Boulanger gave an evening which far exceeded in enjoyment and artistic merit any affair of the kind I have attended since I have been in Paris. Mlle. Boulanger has a pipe organ in her apartment, upon which she plays and teaches. That she is a thorough artist will be understood from the following programme, which she arranged for the entertainment of seventy or seventy five guests, among whom were numbered many prominent musicians.... [The program included music by Bach, Mozart, Pugno, Debussy, N. Boulanger, Fauré, Pierné, and Guilmant.]

This is an unusual programme and was unusually well performed. It was devoted chiefly to the modern French school and it must be admitted that the French have been writing much interesting music, which has aroused criticism both favorable and adverse. The Debussy Quartet may be cited as an example. Debussy is an impressionist. If he were a painter we should probably have purple cows and green, very green grass from his brush, but from the distance the cows would look quite real and the grass very natural, and so we must listen to Debussy's music with the idea rather of gaining an impression than of hearing music based on the traditional rules of harmony and form. Debussy's music should not be put under a microscope; it must be *sensed*, not *listened to*....

Mlle. Boulanger, too, is steeped with the idea of the impressionism of music, and her two songs ["Soleils Couchants" and "Elegie"] are beautiful examples of how far music can arouse mental pictures. Mlle. Boulanger is one of the most talented women of France and much is expected from her pen, and judging from her two songs we shall not be disappointed.[6]

Although Marion's primary lessons were with Pugno and Boulanger, she studied orchestration with Pierre Monteux (1875–1964), whose collaborations with Debussy, Ravel, and Stravinsky would become legendary. She also studied music theory with Louis Campbell-Tipton (1877–1921), who was an American composer living in Paris.[7] Marion was a tireless communicator who maintained these early French connections. Her considerable social skills, like those of her father and Emilie Frances, were a significant professional asset. Colleagues and friends invariably remarked, "Marion knew *everyone*."[8]

Marion's First Widely Celebrated Composition

When Marion returned to New York after her year in Paris, she resumed teaching privately; at this point, she taught both piano and harmony.[9] Marion continued her own piano studies with Eugene Heffley (1862–1925). She commented, "Heffley was one of those rare personalities who knew how to encourage and at the same time evaluate critically. Although he was a teacher of piano, what I learned from him went into my compositions. His studio was a center for contemporary piano music. In fact, in that studio his pupils gave the first recital of Debussy works, probably, to take place in New York."[10] Marion also worked with Walter Henry Rothwell (1872–1927), a conductor who was a close family friend of the Bauer sisters'.[11] Rothwell had recently conducted the first American performances of Wagner's *Parsifal* and Puccini's *Madama Butterfly*. He would later become the first conductor of the Los Angeles Philharmonic.[12] He "gave [Marion] 'musical problems' to solve and helped her to work them out."[13] Rothwell provided Marion with advice and career guidance, a role perhaps just as important as being her piano teacher. He was a musical father to her, even though he was only ten years older.

Marion's next composition provides ample evidence of the success of these studies with Heffley and Rothwell. She composed "Light" in 1907–1908 and published it in 1910. It was dedicated to and frequently sung by Ernestine Schumann-Heink (1861–1936)––a singer characterized as a "national legend"––who regularly performed at the Metropolitan Opera and in recitals in New York, as well as throughout the United States and

Susan E. Pickett

Europe.[14] Schumann-Heink was the first famous artist publicly associated with Marion's music. The impact was strong on sales of Marion's music and on her reputation as a composer. The song sold out very quickly, which led to a second printing.[15] The melodic line is engaging and its mood is mesmerizing. Compared with Marion's first two published works, "Light" is significantly more sophisticated and artistic, and it has some impressionist harmonic characteristics. The song begins in A minor, but stays away from conventional cadential patterns and chord progressions, and then ends in C major.

Although the publisher sold many copies of "Light," only two have been located, both of which are in degraded condition, including the above.[16]

The question Marion's composition teachers might have asked at this point is whether she had the ability to sustain and expand the artistry demonstrated in "Light" in longer, more diverse, more complex compositions.

Marion in Berlin

Around 1910, Rothwell encouraged Marion to study in Europe again. He said to her, "You have talent, but you lack the necessary foundation. What you need is to get away from all outside distractions and concentrate on building up ground work in counterpoint and composition."[17] His statement spoke to the issues of length and diversity, but also to a more sophisticated weaving of melody and accompaniment. He suggested that Marion study with Dr. Paul Ertel (1865–1933) in Berlin. With the financial help of Emilie Frances and other family members, Marion followed Rothwell's advice. Madeleine Goss, in her book *Modern Music-Makers*, describes this phase of Marion's education:

> It was a valuable experience for her, though she was disturbed to find in Germany a certain amount of prejudice against American composers in general, and women composers in particular. To the Europeans of 1911, America still seemed a backwoods nation, musically speaking, with little or no individuality in its expression.
>
> Miss Bauer resented this attitude. She knew that in her own country there was a growing reaction against foreign influence, and a reaching out towards an idiom that would be representatively American—not merely a second-rate copy of the European school. Miss Bauer, then in her early twenties [she was actually twenty-nine], wanted to be a part of the new movement; and she was also determined to prove that her sex could hold its own in music as well as in the other arts.
>
> Before leaving Berlin she gave an informal concert of her songs, and these, like all of her music, were characterized by a breadth and vigor usually thought of as masculine in character.[18]

Compositions by women that were not simple, charming, graceful, easily accessible parlor pieces were frequently characterized as "masculine." According to the music historian Audrey Coulthurst, "This presented a problem, because describing something as feminine was in actuality a very subtle insult rather than a compliment. It hinted at smallness, simplicity, and delicacy, things that were rarely attributed to the work of great masters.

However, using masculine terms denied the composer her own gender, implying that in order to be any good at composition, she could not also be female."[19] Fortunately, from early in her career, Marion was able to shrug off sexist characterizations: "My early aspiration was not to listen to the sly remarks of intolerant men regarding women composers...that if given a reasonable chance for development, an individual talent, regardless of sex, can progress and grow."[20] When Marion returned to New York from Berlin, she had a substantial portfolio of serious art songs, and would seek an American publisher who was willing to take on a woman composer. In the meantime, Emilie Frances traveled to Europe twice, in 1908 and 1910, combining business and pleasure.

Emilie Frances and Debussy

During the first part of Emilie Frances's career as a music critic, Claude Debussy (1862–1918) and Giacomo Puccini (1858–1924) were among the most modern composers. In both cases, Emilie Frances came to know their music and the composers themselves. In her earliest commentary, Emilie Frances did not fully appreciate Debussy's genius:

> Achille Claude Debussy, whose name is scarcely known in America, is of the French school of young composers. He is thirty nine years of age, and he has quite a reputation in his own country. The work [*String Quartet*] is not by any means ordinary, and contains much that is really beautiful, but as is the case with other works coming from the same school, it is complex and full of strange and not altogether agreeable harmonies. To follow this music is too much like climbing over rocky mountains to find that, which after all, might have been given to us at the base of the mountain instead of at the peak.[21]

A few years later, however, we see that she had come to tremendously admire his music, and to understand his position at the threshold of modernism:

We...are thrilled and held, moved to tears and to unfathomable grief by something beyond the story. Is this the realm of Debussy's music or is this the world of the mystic and mysterious? It is intoxicating music; it is maddening because of its indefiniteness; it is elusive as the air, and while it may be true that we do not carry away entire melodies we take with us a complete musical impression of the work. "Pelleas et Melisande" is not to be judged by other standards. It is of itself and in itself, not leaning upon any school or upon any theory.... There are moments of descriptive music, music which is actually meant to represent the drips or flow of water, whispers of the wind through the trees or through the caves. But these are the exceptions, the general rule being shifting tonalities, wandering melodies that are hardly coherent enough to be called melodies, a fair adherence to rhythms and an atmosphere which is almost as effective as the *leit motiv* used by Wagner. There are several climaxes, but these are the culmination of inexpressible grief.... There is impending doom from the rise of the curtain to the fall, and the only thing which seems to be resolved into a certainty, is the tragedy at the close.[22]

Emilie Frances traveled throughout Europe in 1908 and 1910, and on both occasions she interviewed Debussy. She was the first American to whom he granted an interview. Emilie Frances's account allows the reader to envision Debussy's personality and surroundings:

The success in New York, last season, of Claude Debussy's remarkable music-drama *Pelléas et Mélisande* has made its composer an object of keen interest to Americans, and I consider myself privileged in having secured the first interview with the unapproachable and eccentric Mr. Debussy that has been vouchsafed.

Surrounded by luxury which bespeaks originality, this singular Frenchman spends most of his time within the four walls of his interesting workshop, a large room lined with books and hung with pictures, a close scrutiny of which further accentuates the personal tastes of a man of genius. Debussy acknowledged to the writer his aversion to meeting foreigners as due to his lack of understanding the English and German languages, and to his nervousness when the French language does not flow easily.

"It takes too much out of me, and means nothing either to me or to my visitor." I expressed surprise that during the hot months Debussy was still to be found hard at work in Paris, a fact which he explained in the following manner:

"You know, people leave their homes to get away from themselves and from their surroundings. I confess that I live only in my surroundings and in myself. I can conceive of no greater pleasure than sitting in my chair at this desk and looking at the walls around me day by day and night after night. In these pictures I do not see what you see; in the trees outside of my window I neither see nor hear what you do. I live in a world of imagination, which is set in motion by something suggested by my intimate surroundings rather than by outside influences, which distract me and give me nothing. I find an exquisite joy when I search deeply in the recesses of myself, and if anything original is to come from me, it can only come that way."

I then saw Debussy differently from the way my imagination had pictured the writer of "Pelleas et Melisande" and that vast symphony entitled "The Sea." He is a man of intense prejudices, and one would be safe in the belief that his self-appreciation is more an admiration for and devotion for his nationality than mere vanity or self-appreciation.

Debussy firmly believes that his music is purely French and he observed that that which is known as French music is quite as much German as it is French, which is to him a cause of regret as far as the purity of the French school is concerned.[23]

Two years later, Emilie Frances interviewed Debussy again. This account feels more relaxed, and her interjections of her private thoughts as she recounts their conversation are amusing:

For those fortunate enough to know Debussy in his home, this eccentric gentleman has infinite charm. His originality keeps one in a constant flutter of wonder as to what he will say next.

One may anticipate what almost any one is going to say if one knows human nature, but this will be sure to work the other way with Debussy. There are several questions that the unique gentleman does not like to be asked. One of them is "How soon will your opera be finished?" Said opera is, of course, "Fall of the House of Usher," "The Devil in the Belfry," or both. I suggested boldly enough that he was a bit lazy. He took me very seriously and said, "Oh, I am not lazy. I work from morning until night, and sometimes in the night, and then my joy is complete when I know that I may tear up everything that I have done, for you know that to me the greatest satisfaction I find in my work is to know that first and foremost it belongs to me, and the public is the last consideration. I work because I have a passion for work, a passion for creating for the love of the thing itself, and I think that while a man may work constantly all his life, he has no right to give the public one half of what he does, because it can not all be of equal merit, in fact I think that if a man have to his credit three great works he has not lived in vain."

"Then," I answered this exacting composer, "you have nothing more to give the world, for your string quartet, 'La Mer' and 'Pelleas et Melisande' all come under the head of masterpieces."

He smiled quietly, and with that French graciousness and exquisite courtesy he said, "That is most kind in you, but I must say in the nature of reproof that I think that all critics are too kind. They allow things to pass which can but damage the cause, with them there are many artists, when as a matter of fact how many true artists can there be?"

I refrained from supplying the answer as I knew that if I only conceded two, he would cut me down to one and a half, and it is the half to which he objects.

He then led to the matter of an American tour himself and said, "You remember the last time that you were here, you said that I should consider an American tour, but it seemed to impossible to me, however, I think you may be right, do you still think the people would care to have me come?"

I hastened to assure him that America was most interested in his work and in him and that he would be a thoroughly welcome visitor. Then he said, "Well, from my statements I can see that a good deal of my music is sold there, and I take it for granted that every one can not know what I want to express, so I have thought that it would be a good idea to show them what I mean and what I want." Again we agreed and he told me his plans and expectations at length, but added that he would not come until the operas were finished, and that even to get ready to come to America he would not hurry, but he would only work when he really wanted to work.

Debussy is a severe critic, a cynic in the most aggressive sense, but he himself is the first one whom he passes under his lash, and if he were only as severe with others as he is with himself it would explain much of what is regarded as unkindness in his attitude toward his colleagues. One thing is certain—and that is, that taken from any phase, Debussy is fascinating, brilliant, forceful, on the one side, and dreamy, fantastic, imaginative and filmy on the other: in short, he is psychologically true to every note of music that we have seen from his pen and brain.[24]

At the time of Debussy's death in 1918, Emilie Frances clearly perceived his eminence. She understood that both musically and historically he had made an indelible mark:

Debussy is dead! This news fell upon musicians and laymen alike with a sense of personal loss. But to those who knew the great Frenchman, who had had the privilege of entrance into his home and particularly into the sacred precincts of the study in which he did his work, it was a real grief....

The world has lost some great masters within these last few years, but for this generation and the one to come it is doubtful if there will be a greater musical figure, a greater influence or a more widely recognized musical genius than that of Claude Debussy.[25]

Emilie Frances and Puccini

While Emilie Frances only gradually recognized Debussy's genius, she was immediately and completely enamored with Puccini's music. She first met Puccini during his 1907 visit to America, and just before he returned to Italy she took the opportunity to interview him (her fluent Italian no doubt an asset):

Puccini sailed for his home Thursday morning, after a visit which according to his own statement was one of the real delights of his life.

"*A rivederci,*" he said, "but not good bye."

Puccini is one of the most delightful visitors that America has enjoyed, and owing to intelligence and personality it was a rare treat to meet him and to know him in even the desultory manner which a limited visit to New York affords.

The night before he sailed, an informal reception was held at the Astor, when he expressed deep gratitude to the press and to the public of this country, not only for the attention accorded him during this visit but also for their attitude toward his works. It was really difficult to realize that one was in the presence of the great genius which had created all the music of "Tosca," "Madam Butterfly," and other exquisitely musical works because of the great simplicity and unassuming manner of the man. His warm, sunny personality seems a true reflection of Italian atmosphere, and he is a picture of health. He is tall, and built in fine proportion, and very far from the emotional, hysterical creature that people usually picture artists and foreign composers to be. In conversation, Puccini said:

"I find the musical taste very remarkable in this country. It is wide, it is eclectic. You will find the opera houses always full, and when I witnessed the audience of the Boston Symphony Orchestra I was deeply impressed, not alone by the remarkable organization, but I think such audiences tell a wonderful story of the conditions in this country...."

He was asked his opinion of Italian music as compared to German opera. He smiled and absolutely refused to discuss it, saying that it was but natural that he would not make comparisons, and in fact he would not discuss the matter at all.

Puccini was much interested in the theaters; in fact he visited almost every play in the city. Of the theatrical situation he said:

"From the first moment I was most deeply absorbed in the theaters. I wanted to understand the real American tastes, and I wanted to see the American in his enjoyment of the drama. I have been…highly entertained; …but alas, I did not find the subject for which I was looking."

"Why did you especially desire an American subject, Signor Puccini?"

"It is not that I desire an American subject, but I want a subject which will appeal to the American. I want to please the American, and in this country, which is not bound by the conventions and the traditions as in Europe, I hoped to find some original idea, and something which has not been treated either in the past or today.… I did enjoy 'The Girl from the Golden West' immensely. The color and the originality, the setting, everything was very beautiful, but it did not offer me any opportunities.…"

He expressed a great desire to return to this country and to travel more extensively, especially to visit the Pacific Coast, or the "Home of the Girl of the Golden West."[26]

The next year he began composing his opera *The Girl of the Golden West*. During Emilie Frances's 1908 trip to Europe, she visited Puccini at his home in Italy. Years later, looking back, Emilie Frances recalled that "he had much to ask and much to hear concerning [California]. Strangely enough, the wooded spot in which his own home nestled was as typically Californian as anything could be and he was as pleased as a child to be informed of the uncanny circumstance."[27]

In December 1910, Puccini's *The Girl of the Golden West* premiered at the Metropolitan Opera; Puccini was present for rehearsals and performances. Emilie Frances visited with Puccini on several occasions during his time in New York. She reported:

> Puccini did not write an American opera and no one scouted the idea that he did more than he, when he saw the first bill boards in front of the Metropolitan announcing "The Girl of the Golden West" as an American opera.

> "American opera!" he cried, aghast. "This is no American opera; it is pure Italian opera," and the bill boards were changed.[28]

Whether Emilie Frances ever saw Puccini again is unclear, but her adoration of his music was unwavering. At the time of his death fourteen years later she wrote, "The news of Puccini's death came like a thunderbolt upon the music lovers the world over."[29]

Emilie Frances and Alessandro Bonci

During both of Emilie Frances's European trips, she vacationed with Alessandro Bonci (1870–1940) and his family, having met in the great Italian tenor in New York when he performed with the Metropolitan Opera and the Manhattan Opera. (Bonci was considered Enrico Caruso's only major rival.) In her short story about her travels with Bonci, reproduced below, we can see her personality more fully, as well as an activity outside of her professional life:

> Being considerably south of Milan, I could not resist the temptation to run in upon Bonci and his delightful family who are spending the summer months in a quaint little seaside resort not far from Loreto, where the tenor has just erected a palace in every particular and he is preparing to occupy it in September.... The Bonci home is equipped with the most modern improvements, and it has not only five bathrooms, but each bedroom has its adjoining

dressing room with extra supply of special tubs and stands. Electric lights throughout, a roof garden, marble stairways in the front and in the rear of the house from the basement to the roof, all tell the story of what Mr. and Mrs. Bonci have absorbed in the way of appreciation of comforts in America, the land of luxurious living....

The inhabitants [of the village] are exclusively fisher folk who live here as though it were a world of two centuries ago. The boats go out and they come back, and each day history repeats itself with painful precision to those unable to appreciate the wonderful privilege of finding such primitive life in 1910.... There are some few things which I felt that I had seen for the first time in these surroundings—one of these is a storm. We may see the city with its hurrying, scurrying population under the umbrellas, under the eaves of the houses, the lightning may flash and the thunder roar, but until one has witnessed a storm among the people who live on the wave, until one has heard the pitiful sobs of the women and children who wait on the shores, until one has seen the pulling in of the boats from the lashing and the beating of the sea, until one has seen the heavens ablaze with flashes, and heard the reverberations of thunder drown the shrieks of the women, one has little conception of a real storm....

There is no greater excitement in this seaport than that occasioned by the passing of Bonci's enormous touring car through what, for the want of another name, are called streets. Indeed, one of the most extraordinary experiences I have ever enjoyed was an automobile tour that I made with Mr. Bonci and his family from here to Milan and back....

All along the road, as he became recognized even under the real masks which we wore as protection against the dust, could be heard cries of "Ecco Bonci!" ("There is Bonci!"), "Eviva Bonci" ("Long live Bonci!"), indeed were one traveling with a regal party it would be impossible for greater homage, greater affection and greater appreciation of his presence to be manifested.

No more memorable trip has ever been made by your correspondent; indeed, I felt as though no one can know Italy unless one is able to drive through the streets of the tiny villages in this way.... And the streets are so narrow that it seemed almost like driving a car through the hallway of a New York apartment. Also, I will confide to the gentle reader who is many, many miles from Mr. Bonci, that there was another reason why I was so happy to pass through the tiny cities––it was always necessary to slow down, and this always gave me a fresh chance to get a grip on something by which I could hold myself in the car. Talk about speed limit! The fifty-horse machine went at the rate of what seemed like a hundred miles a minute! It must, however, be understood that the dangers are not so great as a speed of this sort would be in America, as the roads lie straight before you and you can see as far as the eye's capacity permits. In addition to this there are no cross-roads. When things arrived at the point where I felt that I had to say something, I gasped between miles, "Say, Mr. Bonci, you won't forget that you are going to make an American tour in concert this season!"

He did not quite get my meaning and asked what I meant, and I explained: "Well, you know, if this things [sic] explodes, or you should happen to meet something, or any one of several things which might happen, did happen, there would be a lot of engagements which would never be filled." He got the idea and said to the chauffeur, "Piano, Piano," which means, as it does in music, "Softly, Softly." We went "piano" for about one minute. Then we began again, going crescendo, CRESCENDO, finally forte, forte, until we were going fortissimo con fuoco and prestissimo brilliante. Get your musical dictionaries if you must, for I really can't stop to explain.

Well, it would seem unkind if I were to tell how much rest I got out of the few moments when they had to put on a new tire. It was an expensive stop, to be sure, but my veil needed adjusting and to be truthful, I needed adjusting. They never could understand just what caused the puncture, but I felt convinced that it was pure suggestion. The shadows of the tall pine trees fell across the road like great poles, and at the speed we were going they made me feel the bumps which were not there, so it was but natural to believe that some of those needles did the mischief. At any rate, it was a rest that I, if no other member of the party, knew how to appreciate.[30]

This extended excerpt gives us a glimpse of Emilie Frances in a more relaxed atmosphere. We are privy to her sense of adventure, and her humor. Also, we are able to appreciate Emilie Frances's dramatic literary style: her ability to paint a landscape, and then bring the people and events within that landscape to life. Moreover, we are reminded of a couple of inventions at that time that affected so many around the world: electric lights and automobiles. They represent mechanical modernism, just as Debussy and Puccini represent musical modernism.

Following this adventure, Emilie Frances boarded the SS *Grosser Furfürst* at Bremen, Germany, and headed back to America. It is amusing that, like Marion, Emilie Frances occasionally fibbed about her age. The ship's log states that she was forty years old, whereas she was actually forty-five.[31]

---

[1]   Goss, *Modern Music-Makers*, 131. She left for Europe in late May or June 1906.

[2]   Ewen, *Composers of Today*, 16.

[3] Marion Bauer, will dated 29 June 1955, proved 17 October 1955, no. 10178. Further details on the document are unreadable. She died 9 August 1955.

[4] Ewen, *Composers of Today,* 16.

[5] Goss, *Modern Music-Makers*, 131.

[6] Marion Bauer, "A Letter from Paris," *MLCG* 13/4 (24 Jan 1907), 5. The article was signed "M. B." It can be inferred that this is Marion Bauer. The entire program was provided in the article, but is abbreviated herein.

[7] Allan MacFarlane, "Paris," *MLCG* 13/12 (6 June 1907), 11.

[8] Jonathan Sternberg, conversation with author, 23 June 2006; Martin Bernstein, conversation with author, 11 Oct 1991.

[9] "Marion Bauer's Pupils," *MLCG* 15/21 (7 May 1908), 6.

[10] Marion Bauer, "Charles T. Griffes as I Remember Him," *MQ* 29/3 (July 1943): 366.

[11] Goss, *Modern Music-Makers*, 131.

[12] Judith Rosen, "Rothwell, Walter Henry," *Grove Music Online*, ed. L. Macy, http://www.grovemusic.com (accessed 2 Aug 2006).

[13] Goss, *Modern Music-Makers*, 131. Rothwell conducted the St. Paul Symphony Orchestra from 1908–1915, so Bauer's studies with him at that time were either sporadic or by correspondence.

[14] Desmond Shawe-Taylor, "Schumann-Heink, Ernestine," *Grove Music Online*, ed. L. Macy, http://www.grovemusic.com (accessed 21 July 2006).

[15] "Unusual Success of Bauer Composition," *ML* 22/7 (17 Aug 1911), 4.

[16] More information about this composition is found in Appendix 1. Complete information is found at marionbauer.org.

[17] Goss, *Modern Music-Makers*, 131.

[18] Goss, *Modern Music-Makers*, 131–132.

[19] Audrey Coulthurst, "The Woman Composer: Gendered Musical Aesthetics and Criticism 1880–1920" (bachelor's thesis, Whitman College, 2004), 19.

[20] Irwin Bazelon, "Woman with a Symphony," *The Baton* of the Phi Beta Fraternity 30/3 (Mar 1951): 6.

[21] Emilie Frances Bauer, "The Kneisel Quartet," *ML* 3/14 (3 Apr 1902), 4.

[22] Emilie Frances Bauer, "Pelleas et Melisande Production," *ML* 15/9 (27 Feb 1908), 7.

[23] Emilie Frances Bauer, "Debussy Talks of His Music," *MLCG* 16/16 (15 Oct 1908), 12. Her *Harper's* interview was reprinted in *The Musical Leader and Concert Goer.*

[24] Emilie Frances Bauer, "Debussy at Home––Some Americans Abroad," *ML* 20/12 (22 Sep 1910), 6.

[25] Emilie Frances Bauer, "Music in New York," *ML* 35/14 (4 Apr 1918), 371.

[26] Emilie Frances Bauer, "A Chat With Puccini," *MLCG* 13/10 (7 Mar 1907), 7.

27   Emilie Frances Bauer, "The Passing of a Great Man," *ML* 48/23 (4 Dec 1924), 535.

28   Emilie Frances Bauer, "Premiere of Puccini's New Opera, 'The Girl of the Golden West,'" *ML* 20/24 (15 Dec 1910), 9–10.

29   Emilie Frances Bauer, "The Passing of a Great Man," *ML* 48/23 (4 Dec 1924), 535.

30   Emilie Frances Bauer, "Emilie Frances Bauer Tells of a Visit to Bonci and an Automobile Tour Through Italy," *ML* 20/15 (13 Oct 1910), 8-9.

31   List or Manifest of Alien Passengers, SS *Grosser Kurfürst*, 17 Sep 1910, http://ancestry.com (accessed 2 June 2007).

CHAPTER 3

MODERNISM

When Marion returned to the United States after a year of studies with Paul Ertel in Berlin, she showed her latest works to two major publishers: G. Schirmer in New York and Arthur P. Schmidt in Boston. Publication with one of these prestigious firms would mean wider distribution of her music, and critical reviews of it in journals. Indeed, Schirmer published two of her songs. Shortly thereafter Schmidt offered Marion an exclusive seven-year contract. Should she accept the offer, Marion would be obligated to seek Schmidt's permission to show any of her works to other publishers. In addition, publication of her works would not be guaranteed and she would feel pressure to compose some pedagogical works because, in the words of Adrienne Fried Block, Schmidt was "insistent that composers also produce educational music, on which the business increasingly depended."[1] Marion and Emilie Frances probably weighed the pros and cons of the exclusive contractual obligations, and then ultimately accepted the offer, perhaps out of admiration for Schmidt's reputation for supporting American composers--both men and women.[2] Schmidt immediately published seven of Marion's songs.

Correspondence between Schmidt and Marion was personal. His letters to Marion have not been preserved, but a substantial number of hers, invariably addressed to "My Dear Mr. Schmidt," offer a wealth of information about Marion's compositions, which of her own works she admired the most, who was performing them, Schmidt's expectations of her, as well as personal information and anecdotes.

Susan E. Pickett

Stars of the Metropolitan Opera began to include Marion's songs in recitals, such as Putnam Griswold (1875–1914), William Wade Hinshaw (1867–1947), Eleonora de Cisneros (1878–1934), Alma Gluck (1884–1938), Maurice Renaud (1860–1933), Clarence Whitehill (1871–1932), Julia Claussen (1879–1941), and Johanna Gadski (1872–1932), among many others. Marion regularly informed Schmidt about which singers were performing particular songs––facts that were constantly updated and published with each new piece. Critics' reviews of her early songs were positive overall, although not effusive: "Marion Bauer, a New York composer, is shown as an ultra-modernist in four songs.... 'The Red Man's Requiem' possesses a good deal of atmosphere and a harmonic background that is, at any rate, suitable to the character of the song.... It abounds in Debussyisms and other traits of modern France."[3]

Several of the songs Marion composed in Berlin, which Schmidt subsequently published, were significantly different in style from her earlier works: she delved into musical modernism, although it is fair to say that initially she had one foot in the nineteenth century and the other foot in the twentieth.

One of the revolutionary changes defining musical modernism was its break from tonality: turning away from melodies and harmonies constructed exclusively from major and minor scales. Instead, composers like Debussy, Ravel, Marion Bauer, Charles Griffes, and many others, were drawn to exotic scales (like the whole tone and pentatonic scales), while they also looked back to medieval modes, all of which generated a new palette of melodic and harmonic sounds. This shook the very foundation upon which centuries of Western music had been built.

One advantage of using medieval modes and exotic scales was that, while the music indeed sounded fresh and different, there were enough similarities with tonal music that the listener also heard something familiar.[4] In her song, "The Red Man's Requiem," the medieval dorian mode renders the song plaintive, regal, and primal. The absolutely insistent rhythmic repetition in the left hand part of the piano accompaniment gives the piece an eerie cohesion: it sounds like a beating drum. Emilie Frances wrote the text for "The Red Man's Requiem," which portrays the decimation of Native Americans. When the text asks, "But where are the bones of the Red Man that the forests used to know?" suddenly the drum stops beating, as if to give the listener a moment to ponder the question. On the title page, Marion indicated, "To the memory of Chief Joseph" (1840–1904), who was a Nez Perce chief in northeastern Oregon, not far from Walla Walla. The song was also dedicated to Putnam Griswold, a Metropolitan Opera bass-baritone, who performed it frequently. "The Red Man's Requiem" may sound tame to twenty-first century ears, but at the time of its release, it was widely labeled "ultra-modern" by several music critics. That label was not necessarily pejorative, but instead could be thought of as a warning sign––Caution: Modernism Enclosed.

Opening measures of "The Red Man's Requiem."[5]

Marion's ability to woo the best performers into seriously considering her so-called "ultra-modern" songs was crucial. Good reviews in respected journals were helpful toward that end. So were Marion's own powers of persuasion: she relentlessly approached performers, often providing them with free copies of her music. She often dedicated her songs to renowned singers who might, then, feel some obligation to perform them. Also, Emilie Frances's efforts in regard to Marion's budding career should not be overlooked. During Marion's year in Berlin, for example, Emilie Frances kept Marion's music and name in the public eye by noting Marion's accomplishments in *The Musical Leader* and reviewing recitals at which Marion's works were performed.

Maud Powell

One acquaintance of both Marion's and Emilie Frances's was the great American violinist Maud Powell (1867–1920), who in 1912 commissioned Marion to write a work for violin and piano. Marion recalled:

> Maud Powell lived across the hall from us a few years ago, and we became very good friends. She had great faith in my ability and often said, "I want you to do for the American composer what I have tried to do for the American woman violinist." She always urged me to write something for her, and I always demurred, saying, "Wait until I have the inspiration." One day I met her on the street, and she said, "You must come up with me. I want to tell you about a wonderful experience I had a few days ago." I went with her to her apartment, and there she told me about a night trip she had made up the mysterious Ocklawaha River in the Florida Everglades; that the grotesque weavings of the thick Spanish moss about the trunks and on long tree branches had cast gloomy, ominous shadows and that on the upper deck of the boat they had built a fire of pine-knots to dissipate the gloom, and when the flames shot up and illumined the scene it was at once grand and awful. She described it with such earnestness that I was deeply impressed with the picture which had been forming itself into the musical images in my mind ever since she had begun to talk. I went to my rooms and immediately set

to work at the piece, having a theme knocking insistently at my head. And so, a few hours later, I went back to her and showed her the almost completed sketches. There were tears in her eyes when she handed it back to me and said, "It is just as though you had been there." So she played it and it was really hers.[6]

Powell described *Up the Ocklawaha* as a "new work which is of an elaborate nature, although it is not a suite and it is not a rhapsody or fantasy. I would almost call it a tone picture, taking into consideration the story that called it into being."[7] Powell also said, "It is probably as good a piece of programme music as has ever been penned. It is extraordinary in its literary quality, if one may say so, reproducing with a rare imaginative power, the weird strangeness of the Ocklawaha River Country. The work is conceived in ultra-modern spirit, and will undoubtedly fall strangely on the ears of some, yet it is so individual in its musical speech, penned with such sure intent, that it must hold a unique place in violin literature."[8]

The American composer Arthur Foote (1853–1937) exclaimed, "[*Up the Ocklawaha*] is the best piece of descriptive music I ever heard!"[9] An anonymous review in *Musical America* was equally enthusiastic:

> It is decidedly one of the most interesting compositions that have come to hand recently. Miss Bauer, whose music is always poetic, has perhaps done her most significant work to date in this composition. No one who read Mme. Powell's suggestive lines can fail to realize that a musical picture of this scene must be, first and last, atmospheric. And Miss Bauer has provided this most admirably. Ultra-modernism is called upon as the means of expression and it administers its duty most capably.
>
> One cannot describe a composition of this type in detail; for it defies more than a general recording of its character. Altered harmonies, biting dissonances, sequences which though a bit harsh at first melt later on the ear, are all

employed and managed in musicianly manner. The scheme is free, the tempo changing frequently; for the mood is pictured faithfully and convention thrown to the winds.

Miss Bauer deserves a wide hearing as the creator of this individual picture in tone. It is by the far the biggest thing she has done that has come to the notice of the present writer and proves her a musician of imaginative power. The music is deep-breathed, far-reaching, eloquent at times, …and always broad and big.[10]

Soon after it was composed, Maud Powell performed it in a New York drawing room, and among the audience members were the Flonzaley Quartet, plus the conductor Alfred Hertz, and violinists Olive Mead and David Mannes. They were so intrigued that they asked Powell to play it again.[11]

The composition has impressionistic characteristics, including the use of parallel chords, extended tertian harmony, the use of the full range of the keyboard for color, harmonics in the violin part, and a depiction of nature. Marion showed no fear of dissonance, and was drawn to the new harmonies championed by the impressionists, though she juxtaposed them with somewhat more conventional sounds. However, her penchant for a strong melodic line, aural beat-clarity, and dark timbres morphed the piece into a style that was distinctive. Her first work for violin is technically idiomatic, as though a violinist wrote it. Schmidt published it in 1913, adorned with a cover designed by Marion.[12]

Cover of *Up the Ocklawaha* (woodcut designed by Marion Bauer).[13]

Opening of *Up the Ocklawaha*. Maud Powell's poem is at the top.[14]

In 1913, Schmidt also published Marion's pedagogical works for piano, *In the Country: Four Little Piano Pieces*. Although Marion's primary compositional focus throughout her career was art music, she would occasionally compose teaching pieces, in part because Schmidt expected his composers to do so. She also wanted a fresh repertoire for her own students. Why did she write these works in such a conservative style, unlike her non-pedagogical works? Again, that is probably what Schmidt expected or demanded. (Some of Marion's post-Schmidt pedagogical works are much more modern.)

Marion's Wars

In June 1914, Marion went to Europe for further studies with Paul Ertel in Berlin.[15] Her previous stint with Ertel was notable, as that was when Marion first delved into modernism. This time she planned to study orchestration with him––five lessons a week. Marion had less than two months of study before World War I commenced. Marion sent a cable to Emilie Frances on 2 August 1914 stating that she "was still in Berlin awaiting the first opportunity to get out."[16] Emilie Frances immediately wrote a letter to the editor of *The New York Times*: "With the great German vessels lying in our ports unable to move out, and likely to remain indefinitely, with 100,000 of our nearest and dearest visiting in Germany and all over Europe, could it not be possible for the American Government to buy these boats from their Governments and own them for the future seafaring which will eventually fall to the lot of this country? This would be a more reasonable way of settling the matter than to leave the present agonizing question open of the fate of those who are now tied up in Berlin unable to get away."[17] Emilie Frances's fear for Marion's safety is palpable. Marion's residence was in the heart of Berlin,[18] where crowds gathered, singing German war songs––"Was blasen die Trompeten?"––as infantry and cavalry passed through.[19] On the same day Emilie Frances wrote her letter, a war correspondent in Berlin reported, "Every moment a new rumour whirled through the maddened city. Every hour a new edition of the papers appeared." Guns were mounted on public buildings and cathedrals. Foreigners were stopped and searched innumerable times, and sometimes held for hours of questioning.[20] Passenger ships were filled beyond capacity then sailed from Antwerp to America under blackout conditions through waters teeming with war ships: "On the steamer...it was impossible to get the face value of American money...[and] the heaviest burden was being felt by thousands of American women who had gone abroad with no margin of expense, and who were now practically penniless."[21] *The Musical Leader* reported that Marion had "some thrilling experiences in her escape from the German capital,"[22] but didn't elaborate on how she managed to get to London where she boarded the *Virginian*, which was headed to Montreal, Canada. Baggage was limited on both trains and boats, and Emilie Frances reported that Marion's only concern was the luggage that contained her manuscripts,[23] which, in the end, was nearly all she was allowed to bring with her.[24] (Amy Beach was also in Germany when the war broke out. Some of her manuscripts were lost when her baggage was "dumped in a heap at the side of the road miles out in the country in order to make room for a company of soldiers.")[25] Emilie Frances commented in *The Musical Leader* on the younger American students who were hurriedly returning home:

> Nothing...is more shocking than to see some of the young girls who have been utterly and absolutely alone, drifting about Europe. Among those returning are girls not more than fifteen years of age, who have been alone in the large centers of Europe, where they have fondly deluded themselves that they were getting better instruction than in America. The folly of this amounts almost to an insanity, and if this outbreak will cause parents and guardians to be brought to their senses on this subject it can not be said that it has been in vain....
>
> It is a fact that Europe is swarming with young girls, a terrifying percentage of whom are under twenty, and in this crisis the situation is utterly beyond conception. Many of them may be saved from worse fates than that through which they have just passed, by the compulsory return to their own country. Needless to say that a new era has dawned for the education of our people as it has for many other phases of life in America.[26]

For the next several weeks, Emilie Frances's essays focused on how the war might affect music in America, especially with the absence of foreign soloists, conductors, and teachers (some of whom were called into military service in their own countries). One professional change did occur for

Emilie Frances at the outbreak of the war: she "severed her connections" with the *New York Evening Mail*, for which she had been music critic for six years.[27] Why she did so is unknown, but the terse manner in which she announced it sounds acrimonious.

Marion's next letter to Schmidt, written three months after her return to America, does not allude to the preceding summer. If she had faced terrifying circumstances, she hadn't lost her sense of humor, as we see in her letter regarding her new song: "Marie Morrisey had a splendid success with 'Only of Thee and Me' last Monday––she had to repeat it. It is to be sung again...at the Century Opera Company 'with the composer (trembling in her boots) at the piano.'"[28] With the onset of World War I, Walter Rothwell's orchestra in St. Paul, Minnesota, disbanded. He moved back to New York City, where Marion began to work regularly with him. She commented that she "received some of my most valuable training during these years of war."[29]

Schmidt now published several of Marion's more conservative songs, such as "Only of Thee and Me." It is dedicated to Mrs. Cecil H. Bauer (Rose Bloch Bauer). Schmidt also published "A Little Lane," "Phyllis," and "Youth Comes Dancing O'er the Meadow." A review in *The Musical Leader,* possibly written by Emilie Frances, stated, "The new songs are written in a genial spirit and are, perhaps, more than her older ones, within the grasp of the average singer, while losing none of their dignity or musical value."[30] There is little doubt that Marion felt obligated to provide Schmidt with some songs in this vein. Schmidt also pressed Marion to get those songs performed in order to increase sales of her music. Marion found one custom particularly disgusting: composers paying singers to perform their songs. When Schmidt passed along one such suggestion from a professional singer, Marion responded indignantly:

> As far as Mme. [Mariska] Aldrich's proposition is concerned, I do not know just what to say. I have very little money to spend in that way, and I never yet have paid anyone to sing any of my songs. If she were to have a program of songs of your [Schmidt's] publication or even

a program of women's compositions I should not like to appear 'offish' or 'up-ish'––and if the proposition were to obligate one's self for the sale of twenty tickets or so I might considerate [sic] it, but under ordinary circumstances I would not establish a precedent, it is not to my mind a good thing to do, for it would readily lead to the point when singers would only sing such songs as they were paid for, and I feel that it would be disastrous at a time when singers are just beginning to realize the absolute necessity of singing English songs. Besides which, when I shall be financially in the position to do so, I want to choose my own singers and give my own recital in Aeolian Hall.[31]

In a similar vein, Marion commented, "I also promised Mabel Garrison [Metropolitan Opera soprano] some of my songs.... She felt quite hurt that I never had <u>asked</u> her to sing my songs! Singers are queer birds, but don't tell anyone that I said so."[32]

In 1915[33] and 1916[34] two all-Bauer recitals were presented in New York City. Several of her recent songs–– "Orientale," "By the Indus," "The Minstrel of Romance," and "Das Erdenlied"––were performed by the renowned singers May Dearborn-Schwab, Mary Jordan, and Elsa Alves, with Marion as the accompanist.[35] A glowing review of the 1916 recital was published in *The Musical Leader*:

A program of twenty songs by Marion Bauer was given Saturday afternoon in Chickering Hall.... Perhaps the most dramatic number of the program was a setting of an oriental poem by Cale Young Rice, "By the Indus," in which both the composer and the singer achieved an emphatic success.... Mr. Hunter's baritone voice of clear quality, excellent attack and fine resonance lent itself well to a number of the virile songs which have made Miss Bauer's compositions most valuable to baritones in search of "manly" numbers....

> Miss Bauer played her own accompaniments with the sympathy which can only be supplied by the composer and a very large audience accorded her and the singers untiring testimony of appreciation.[36]

Marion sent her new songs to Schmidt. Although he had retired in 1916, whereupon H. R. Austin and two other employees took over the daily operations of the company, Schmidt remained active as a consultant and continued as Marion's primary contact. Her letters to Schmidt continued for two more years, but gradually took on a different mood. Reading between Marion's lines, we can see that Schmidt had become unhappy with aspects of her new compositions:

> I'm sorry you don't "see" "By the Indus" and "Fair Goes the Dancing" ["Orientale"].... Several of the singers have been at my sister to get "By the Indus" for their programs, and it is one of the best songs I ever wrote to my thinking and also to the thinking of many people who have seen the song.

> I can't always write the same kind of song—I have read at least a thousand poems—to try to find the kind of lyric you would like but it isn't written any more as much as it used to be.

> I want to talk it all over with you. I'm afraid your last letter discouraged me.[37]

Marion's progressing modernism was likely part of Schmidt's concern, and the letter also indicates he was not happy with the texts she chose. We learn that Marion's unpublished songs were being presented in recital, which allowed her to hear polished public presentations prior to publication. The performers would give Marion feedback, enabling her to make changes before submitting the manuscripts to a publisher. Performers who were in the audience would often express interest in the music, so Marion would provide manuscripts to them, which had the ripple effect of getting her unpublished music known. Effusive audience reactions and positive comments from well-known performers presumably provided leverage with Schmidt. The same year that tension first arose between Marion and Schmidt, encouraging reviews in *The Musical Leader* provide a stark contrast to the tone of their correspondence:

> Marion Bauer, the New York composer whose songs are being sung by the great artists and who is quickly achieving fame, was in Chicago (en route to Portland) for a few hours.

> It is this same Marion Bauer who in a few years has come to the front and won recognition for creative ability as well as for highest musicianship, and now publishers are writing to her, so there is no necessity for the customary begging, of which the average composer has to be guilty.[38]

Throughout the year, the magazine reviewed numerous recitals in which renowned singers, such as Marcella Craft, included Marion's songs. Perhaps the simultaneity of problems with Schmidt and the public praise offered by *The Musical Leader* was coincidental. It is more plausible that Emilie Frances and her colleagues at the magazine were applying public pressure on Schmidt. The comment in *The Musical Leader* about other publishers writing to Marion could certainly be construed as a shot across the bow to Schmidt, though admittedly neither Marion's nor Emilie Frances's correspondence alludes to the matter. Marion's next letter to Schmidt is slightly apologetic, while still asserting independence: "I hope to do what you wish, and I hope I may produce the kind of work that will make you feel that your confidence has not been misplaced. Composing at best is experimental and must be spontaneous. It always has been so with me and I always feel that I am still in the formative period of my work. My studying is not over by any means, and the leisure I feel I may take for at least the next few months will give me the opportunity to study and grow, and I hope unfold."[39] Ultimately, Schmidt did publish "By the Indus" and "Orientale." Whether he caved in to the pressure or had a change of heart about the songs is not known.

The text of "By the Indus," by Cale Young Rice, paints a scene at the bank of the Indus River in Pakistan, where a woman waits in vain for her lover. In this song, Marion found her mature modern voice. She skillfully created a cohesive song filled with drama and poignancy. One music critic praised the song as "dramatic and rich in color."[40] Listening with twenty-first century ears, it is hard to imagine what Schmidt's objections might have been. Perhaps Marion had crossed his threshold of tolerance for modern harmonies. In any case, the musical result is in a ubiquitously modern and unified harmonic style.

Marion's Personal Reflections

Marion's letters to Schmidt occasionally include comments about personal family matters and tragedies, and sometimes reveal humor, such as the following excerpts from 1916 and 1917, respectively:

> I have just had a delightful week visiting at the seashore, playing golf, motoring, swimming and going in surf bathing. Does this all sound very giddy for me?[41]

> I was sorry to have been so far away in September…but at that time I was falling in love with Santa Barbara and the Grand Canyon, which made a very deep impression on me. (I feel in love with <u>places</u>, not <u>people</u>, you will observe.)[42]

Marion and Emilie Frances's brother, Cecil, died around this time, and Marion's usually optimistic and effervescent letters changed in mood as she grieved. Given that his death occurred at the height of the tensions between Marion and Schmidt, this was an exceptionally difficult time for Marion, both personally and professionally:

> I had been worrying about my debt to you––that is, not the debt itself, but the fact that I had not produced the work that you had hoped for, and it is a keen sorrow to me that I have been a disappointment to you.

It is not stubbornness on my part not to write simple
things––I can only write what I feel––and someday (soon
I hope) I shall learn to do the big simple thing. I must do
my work in steps––evolutionary, not revolutionary. I have
so little time to write that naturally change of style is slow.

I shall soon send you "Night in the Woods" and "A Parable"
in both of which I hope you will find the simplicity and
directness that I tried to put into them.[43]

Schmidt rejected the two songs mentioned in the letter, and also rejected
"Roses Breathe in the Night" and "The Epitaph of a Butterfly." Other
companies published all of the songs three years later. "Night in the
Woods" is arguably the best of the group, with an ethereal mood, a well-
contoured melodic line, and simple but unpredictable harmonies.

Night in the Woods

Opening measures of "Night in the Woods"[44]

Marion's final letter to Schmidt appears to be her response to learning that her exclusive contract would not be renewed: "I can say nothing about your decision except that I must abide by it. I take it for granted that you really don't want the manuscripts and that I am free to show them to anyone else, at any rate I should like your permission to do so.... I think it best to send the mss [manuscripts] to my sister Emilie Frances––also a letter giving me freedom to do as I please with them."[45] Marion wrote this letter to Schmidt from Oregon, where she was visiting friends, and also giving a lecture entitled "The Modern Trend of Art in Music and Its Relation to the War." The *Oregonian* reported on her lecture and captured her thoughts, pleas, and perhaps frustrations: "Miss Bauer played on the piano Debussy and Scriabne [Scriabin] music-scales, and then asked for more sympathy for the thoughts and creations of such representative composers, because they hear sounds we do not hear, and have dreams unknown to us."[46] The absence of an exclusive contract with the Arthur P. Schmidt Company did not preclude Marion from approaching them with subsequent works. They did, in fact, publish a few. Her business correspondence with the company continued, but from this point forward, her letters were addressed to H. R. Austin, Schmidt's successor. Marion's compositional career entered a new phase now, one unencumbered by the conflict between her own creative impulses and Schmidt's limited tastes and pragmatic business concerns.

Emilie Frances and Modernism

Emilie Frances was a music critic living between late romanticism and modernism. On the one hand, she heard Camille Saint-Saëns (1835–1921) perform in New York in 1906, when he was seventy-one years old. She wrote, "It has been a great privilege to meet and to know the personality no less than the equipment of this man who stands in the unique position of being the last of a great school and the first of that in which we find ourselves today, between the past and the present representing the bridge in fact not only for his own country, but for the musical world at large."[47] On the other hand, she came to know Gustav Mahler (1860–1911), who stood at the precipice of modernism. He lived in New York part-time, where from 1907–1911 he conducted the Metropolitan Opera, the New York

Symphony Orchestra, and the New York Philharmonic Orchestra. Mahler received a mixed reception of both his conducting and his compositions. He had to endure rumors about being replaced, scathing reviews in the *New York Tribune*, dwindling audiences, and disgruntled management. Emilie Frances reviewed nearly every concert Mahler conducted in New York. Her reviews were largely glowing, and her admiration for the man, his talent, and his music was unwavering. Here are two excerpts from those reviews:

> He is an unassuming looking man, of somewhat pedagogic appearance, but in his readings there is nothing of this. Instead, there is a highly poetic flow of music, and there are many qualities so subtle as to elude a name for them.[48]

> One does not expect a public to be won so completely at the first hearing of a work as complicated and as open to debate as is the second symphony of the man who has become a heroic figure in our season's music.... The thing that must impress itself forcibly upon the willing listener is the marvelous genius in workmanship in Mahler's score.... As we know him before his orchestra, Mahler is the embodiment of vital force and concentrated energy, and so he has written himself down in every measure.[49]

Early in 1911, while still in America, Mahler's health declined rapidly. He had an infection, for which he sought a remedy in France, to no avail. He was then taken to a sanitarium in Vienna, where he died in May, 1911. Emilie Frances mourned his death:

> Mahler possessed gigantic talent, too great to have been subjected to the whims of a Board of Direction which harassed his musical sense.... Either he wore his hair too long, or he allowed the kettledrums too much license––it matters little, but America formed its own judgment about Mahler.... To those who understood and appreciated Mahler's worth, his colossal musicianship, his

uncompromising sincerity in the highest musical ideals, his inconceivable knowledge, the position that he has left vacant is not possible to fill.[50]

Just as Emilie Frances learned to appreciate modernism in Debussy's music, so too with Mahler's music, which at that time was challenging for many listeners and players alike. She might comment on the extreme length of one of his symphonies, but she would also note that the audience's interest was held throughout. She also immediately knew that his music would be controversial, and she was quick in her denunciation of the rancor and pettiness that swirled around both Mahler and his music. (Marion, too, was enchanted by Mahler's music. She characterized his eighth symphony as "one of the most glorious musical utterances I have ever heard.")[51]

It would have been difficult to predict how Emilie Frances would react to the more pungent musical modernism, such as the first atonal compositions by Arnold Schoenberg, or Stravinsky's bitonality. We saw with Debussy's music that she was slightly put off at first, and then came to fully embrace it. Unlike the Parisians who heard the infamous 1913 premiere of Stravinsky's *Le Sacre du Printemps* (The Rite of Spring), Americans had to wait until 1924 to hear the work on their own soil. In the meantime, critics such as Emilie Frances were tantalized by reading about the riot at the premiere of that work, which seems to have created an expectation about what Stravinsky's music might be like. In the interim, other works by Stravinsky were performed in New York, such as his first symphonic work, *Symphony in E-flat*. Emilie Frances reported:

> There must have been extreme disappointment among those who went to the Russian Symphony concert Saturday night at Carnegie Hall, where Modest Altschuler announced the first performance in this country of the first symphony of Strawinsky, whose name stands for everything that is discordant, dissonant and calculated to set one's musical teeth on edge. But there was no such experience for those who sat nerved up for the worst, ready to pounce upon the cacophonist, ready to proclaim

his great superiority over Beethoven, Bach et al. On the contrary, there was all the classic rigidity of an old master who might have written the first two movements and all the color of Tschaikowsky, who in spirit, if not in fact, was responsible for the andante. There is never a lapse from definite form, and worst of all, for those who waited in vain to justify their own departure from form, rhythms, harmonic structure, it proved to be the work of one who was thoroughly schooled in the most scholarly and most classical forms.

However, we must not forget that as in the case of many compositions which here and there drift onto our stages, both concert and operatic, it is a work which we should have heard when Strawinsky was younger and when the work was written, which is over ten years ago. Since that time he has repented of the beauties of his gifts, and he has dipped his pen into the gall of life into the same inkpot as Bakst, Schoenberg, and others of that ilk. However, one can but wonder whether Strawinsky is as black as he is painted. This question comes to mind remembering the excitement which preceded the performance of his sketches for chamber music [*Three Pieces for String Quartet*], played recently by the Flonzaley Quartet. It is true that they were written in the ultra-modern, cubist, formless, futurist school which may mean much and may mean nothing, but, nevertheless, those who expected great cannonading, bombs, and loud detonations, felt at the conclusion that all had failed to touch powder save one small fire-cracker.[52]

American music critics were at a disadvantage because they were hearing Stravinsky's stylistic metamorphoses out of order, so to speak. In the meantime, Americans read volumes about the European premieres of his controversial works, without being able to judge for themselves. Emilie Frances perceived correctly that Stravinsky's early symphony (1905-1907; performed in New York in 1916) was conceived very differently than *Le*

Sacre du Printemps, which followed it (1911-1913; performed in New York in 1924). Then his style changed again with his *Three Pieces for String Quartet* (1914; performed in New York in 1916), which was more indicative of his impending neoclassicism. His phenomenal ballets of the interim, however, had not yet been presented in New York.

Within a month of hearing Stravinsky's *String Quartet*, Emilie Frances had the opportunity to see the first American performances by the Ballets Russes, displaying the remarkable collaboration between Serge Diaghilev, impresario of Ballets Russes, and Stravinsky. Several of the legendary dancers in the group performed, including Massine, and the stage settings were by Bakst, Golovine, and Larionow. The program included Stravinsky's *L'Oiseau de Feu* (The Firebird), composed 1909–1910, as well as *The Enchanted Princess*, by Tchaikovsky, and *Soleil de Nuit* and *Sheherezade*, by Nikolay Rimsky-Korsakov (1844–1908). Emilie Frances had a mixed reaction to this concert. On the one hand, she thoroughly appreciated Stravinsky's music:

> The program included the exquisitely beautiful ballet, "L'Oiseau de Feu," which is mirrored with marvelous dexterity in the music of Igor Strawinsky and which is Strawinsky in his most modern effects. So fascinating is the stage that one is conscious of the music not as a thing apart, the severe critical analysis is forgotten, some of the musical effects which might otherwise be offensive to more orthodox ears, flit in and out of the score as though merely to remind one that there is an appendix of music, yet so much of it is so completely apart of the thing that delights the eye that one forgets that two senses are involved....

> The composer in every sense showed what a mastery of classical form is his and what a strange power of making one feel color in his harmonies or in his dissonances.... When...the Strawinsky "Fire Bird" music was heard as a component part of the wonderful shift of colors applied

to something tangible, something carrying an interest outside of color per se, something which made the dancers more dazzling and the costumes a living, pulsing art, it became apparent that Strawinsky achieved much that could hardly have been dreamed of by those who believe that the sense of color in musical sound is a "fad" or an affectation.[53]

On the other hand, she agreed with a contingent of people who found some of the choreography unseemly in this performance and other performances that same week (including Diaghilev's production of Debussy's *Prélude à l'après-midi d'un faune*), and welcomed the enforcement of a law that compelled Diaghilev to modify it:

[The Russian Ballet] is a fine organization and it has brought new emotions and appreciation of a novel nature to many. It is a pity, however, that so much of the beauty is wasted upon the licentious side of life. Nothing can be so beautiful as the human form, and in artistic and poetic pantomime the imagination might rove into the loveliest ideals, but there is no modification which could make "Scheherazade" [sic] and several other of the pantomimes and dances anything but just what they are––distinctly nasty. Much sarcasm and many pointed remarks of a supercilious nature were launched at the decent minded people of this community when the law compelled a certain degree of modification. One recalls with anger the bitter manner in which Mr. Diaghileff said when he witnessed a revised performance of the above named work, "America's morals are saved!" It may be well to teach the impresario a few truths about some of America's "prudes" and it were well if the lesson might be learned before the company undertakes a tour through the country. It may be that New York has become sufficiently cosmopolitan to endure all sorts of disgusting exhibitions because, be it understood, New York endures anything rather than go

to the trouble of correcting or removing a nuisance, but
other sections of the country are still sufficiently virile
and energetic to show its repugnance in no uncertain
manner.[54]

Yes, Emilie Frances could be prudish, but she was not alone in being offended
at the blatantly sexual choreography. The Catholic Theatre Movement,
which was a society that censored theatrical presentations by issuing a
"white list" of performances that met with their approval, circulated a
bulletin against the Russian Ballet. Private citizens also objected. The
New York City police department received so many complaints about the
choreography that they sent a contingent to watch the ballet.[55] Diaghilev
then changed the choreography under protest, saying, "The reception
the American public has given the dancers indicates that their taste
is no different from that of European nations, and at the same time
makes ridiculous the attitude of the police."[56] At the end of the modified
performance Diaghilev did indeed say, "America is saved!"[57]

War of Words

Between 1915 and 1923, Emilie Frances wrote several articles about women
composers and American composers, and sometimes both topics combined.
One example is her article about Amy Beach, who had performed a few
times in New York during Emilie Frances's tenure with *The Musical Leader*.
Beach's music—especially her songs for voice and piano—was performed
there often. With the onset of World War I, Beach moved from Europe
back to the United States, and resided briefly in New York. There, she
came to know Emilie Frances and Marion better. Emilie Frances gave
a reception in Beach's honor.[58] She also traveled to Philadelphia to hear
Beach's symphony performed:

> There were those who felt it worth while to go over to
> Philadelphia from New York Friday afternoon when
> Leopold Stokowski [conductor of the Philadelphia
> Orchestra] placed as first number on his program a
> symphony by Mrs. H. H. A. Beach, a work which needs

no excuse because it is from the pen of a woman or an American. It is of sterling worth and will stand upon its own merit, on the other hand there is something to be said in the matter. Every orchestra, with the exception of the Boston Symphony Orchestra, owes its being to the women who are willing to work for the sake of keeping these organizations alive, and as the least thing that the conductors could do in return for the untiring interest with which the women have worked they might include this symphony in their regular programs. Josef Stransky [conductor of the New York Philharmonic Orchestra], who has shown much interest in American compositions would probably do it if he were shown the score, and no doubt Walter Damrosch [conductor of the New York Symphony Orchestra] would do it if even to prove that he was willing to allow woman to stand or fall by her own writing, if we are to believe that he entirely denies woman the powers to create a great musical work. However, to Leopold Stokowski falls the honor of having done the work as he would have done any work, and the reception with which it met must have proven to him that he had not erred in judgment.[59]

Emilie Frances's conjecture, that Joseph Stransky (1872–1936) might have responded favorably to Beach's symphony if he saw the score, was soon refuted by Stransky himself, when he was quoted at length in the *Sun* newspaper about his low opinion of women composers. *The Musical Leader*, in an article about the interview, reprinted much of what Stransky said, and also asked Marion to comment:

With a noble disregard of consequences, Josef Stransky, according to a writer in the New York "Sun," has placed himself on record as saying that women, poor things, had no creative ability. Acquainted with the fact that the interviews of professional interviewers are frequently inaccurate, we are giving Mr. Stransky the benefit of believing that he was misquoted when he said the [sic] "music is a masculine art" and that the great woman composer has yet to come. If Sarah Addington, the "Sun" interviewer, is quoted correctly, then Mr. Stransky is credited or discredited with the following:

From Sappho to Chaminade is a road centuries long, but a road unadorned by musical compositions from the lyre twanged by woman, save at intervals so far apart that they have almost escaped the notice of Time and Fame.

Why should it be so?

Women have sung the songs created by men, they have admittedly inspired them, and yet that same inspiration has passed them by.

And women have done distinguished work in the other arts––in literature, painting, sculpture. Why has the Muse of Music alone evaded them?

It has been suggested that in Darwinism one may find the answer––that the female of the species is not the singer; that, just as in birddom, the lady birds let the gentlemen have all the musical honors, so in the realm of humans the ladies have chosen the role of listeners and granted the gifts of musical creation to the men. But there are other more interesting reasons, the unflattering one offered by Josef Stransky, conductor of the Philharmonic Orchestra, for example, and the encouraging one proffered by Miss Marion Bauer, a composer herself.

Mr. Stransky, polished, gracious gentleman, leaves nothing to be desired in the way of frankness. One might expect him to gloss over the unpoetic realities of this grim world. But not he.

"Women haven't the ability to compose music," says he serenely and with utter suavity; "if they could they would. But they haven't the brains, I suppose."

Gasps from his interviewer. "Do you mean that?"

Mr. Stransky made a gallant gesture––a slow sweep of his cigarette, a deferential move of this head.

"Then why have they not composed?" he asked, pausing for a reply.

The reply was an indefinite murmur concerning "woman's lack of encouragement."

"Encouragement? She has had all the encouragement that men have had. Sophie Mozart was given the same training as her brother, but she only played very beautifully. Besides," Herr Stransky puffed a moment at his cigarette and then went on, "genius will out. If women had the spark there all the king's horses and all the king's men couldn't stamp it out. No, musical competition requires a colossal brain."

The implication went by unchallenged. One accepts slander delivered in such velvet tones and with such courtesy. The next question came meekly.

"Do you think women may begin to compose more and more?"

"I fear so," smiled Mr. Stransky.

He fears so, indeed! Indignation springs eternal.

What insult next to heap upon this injury?

"You see," he explained, "women have shown that they can do only mediocre work in composing. Now we haven't time for mediocrity, have we? So why should I say I would encourage women to compose just because they are women? Certainly, if a woman showed genius, I should help her and urge her on all I could, but because of her gift, not her sex. So far women have lacked personality in music. They ought to develop that quality. Of course, you know that women are composing to some extent, but the great woman composer has yet to come. And I think she won't. Music is a masculine art. Women will never do symphonies; they can do Lieder very nicely."

Woman's sphere again! That was the Stransky verdict.

But Miss Bauer offers the balm to the Stransky wounds. Miss Bauer is a cheerful, energetic person who, like Mr. Stransky, speaks "from the heart out." The two are great friends, by the way, their friendship not in the least interfering with their individual and differing opinions.

"I have all sorts of hope for the woman composer," asserts Miss Bauer. "Why, this is just the beginning of woman's era! Activity for women is in the air now; the woman composer will feel some stimulus to work. No there have been no women Beethovens, but I ask you, how many men Beethovens are there? Not a crowd of them, certainly. If we should count the great musical geniuses that the ages have produced I doubt if we should have more than twenty prominent names. Now, that is not such a bad start on the women, I think. Women in musical composition have a great deal to overcome. They are apt to be superficial and fickle in their work, but they are capable of cultivating depth and stability. Well, now, we just can't say that women are not doing good work. You can hardly see a program that doesn't contain the name of a woman composer."

"Do you think that music is a masculine art?" asked the interviewer, still smarting from the former encounter.

"Yes. But lots of women have masculine minds, and lots of men have nice little effeminate brains. A woman's music will be more emotional than that of a man, but it need not be weaker. Please let me make this very strong: that I think woman can create music and will create music in the very near future. She is doing it now, but we shall not know for a generation just what her work is worth. Time is the only test for masterpieces, even the masterpieces of a woman!"[60]

Marion leaves the reader perplexed by several of her statements. Exactly what she meant by her assertion that music is a masculine art is not clear; though, if she meant that composition was generally associated with men, then that was self-evident. But she seemed to be referring to a particular way of thinking by using the phrase "masculine mind." Did she mean analytical? That is the most likely interpretation, since the stereotype of that era was that men were analytical and women were emotional. Nor is it clear what she meant by her statement that a woman's music was more emotional. How? Is there anything more emotional than the end of Verdi's *La Traviata*? Did she mean that a woman composer would create more of such moments in her own opera? Perhaps she bought into the cliché that women were more emotional than men, and then projected that into artistic creation. Finally, was Marion being flippant when she used the phrase "nice little effeminate brains"? Here we have no doubt.

---

[1]   Adrienne Fried Block, "Arthur P. Schmidt, Music Publisher and Champion of American Women Composers," in *The Musical Woman*, ed. Judith Lang Zaimont. (New York: Greenwood Press, 1984), 151.

2   Block, "Arthur P. Schmidt, Music Publisher and Champion of American Women Composers," 145,

3   A. W. K. [A. Walter Kramer], "New Music––Vocal and Instrumental," *MA* 27/1 (9 Nov 1912): 24.

4   While the use of exotic scales seemed revolutionary in the first decade of the twentieth century, they soon paled in the face of atonality, like that of Schoenberg.

5   More information about this composition is found in Appendix 1. Complete information is found at marionbauer.org.

6   Erminie Kahn, "The Aims of Marion Bauer, Expression of All Moods in Music Sought by Composer Almost Unique in Writing for Piano—Her Scholarly Musicianship," *ML* 39/23 (3 June 1920), 550.

7   Karen Shaffer and Neva Greenwood, *Maud Powell: Pioneer American Violinist* (Arlington, VA: Maud Powell Foundation; Ames, Iowa: Iowa State University Press, 1988), 328.

8   Karen Shaffer, correspondence to author, June 2006. Shaffer quoted from a document found in Maud Powell's archive, but did not specify the source of quotation.

9   Goss, *Modern Music-Makers*, 133.

10   "New Music––Vocal and Instrumental," *MA* 17/25 (26 Apr 1913): 36.

11   "'Up the Ocklawaha,' A Tone Picture," *ML* 25/18 (1 May 1913), 697.

12   Marion Bauer to A. P. Schmidt, 18 Dec 1912.

13   More information about this composition is found in Appendix 1. Complete information is found at marionbauer.org.

14   Ibid.

15   Marion Bauer to A. P. Schmidt, 30 May 1914.

16   "Marion Bauer in Berlin," *ML* 28/6 (6 Aug 1914), 151.

17   Emilie Frances Bauer, letter to the editor, *NYT*, 4 Aug 1914, 10.

18   Marion Bauer to A. P. Schmidt, 30 May 1914. Her Berlin address was Pension Kopplin, Nürnbergerplatz 1.

19   J. W. Nevinson, "Berlin a-Tiptoe for War in Aug 1914," www.greatwardifferent.com/Great_War/German_Portraits/Berlin_1914.htm (accessed 24 July 2006).

20   J. W. Nevinson, "Berlin a-Tiptoe for War in Aug 1914," www.greatwardifferent.com/Great_War/German_Portraits/Berlin_1914.htm (accessed 24 July 2006).

21   *NYT*, "3,600 Refugees Home on 2 Ships," 18 Aug 1914, 5.

22   "Marion Bauer's Songs on Many Programs," *ML* 28/9 (27 Aug 1914), 245.

23   "Marion Bauer Arriving This Week," *ML* 28/8 (20 Aug 1914), 203.

24   "Marion Bauer's Songs on Many Programs," *ML* 28/9 (27 Aug 1914), 245.

25   "Mrs. H. H. A. Beach's Music Lost," *ML* 28/10 (3 Sep 1914), 261.

26   Emilie Frances Bauer, "Music in New York," *ML* 28/9 (27 Aug 1914), 230.

27   Emilie Frances Bauer, "Music in New York," *ML* 28/7 (13 Aug 1914), 174.

28   Marion Bauer to A. P. Schmidt, 13 Nov 1914.

29   Ewen, *Composers of Today,* 16.

30   "New Songs by Marion Bauer," *ML* 28/4 (23 July 1914), 96.

31   Marion Bauer to A. P. Schmidt, 25 Feb 1916.

32   Marion Bauer to A. P. Schmidt, 31 Mar 1918.

33   "Marion Bauer Compositions at Wanamaker's," *ML* 29/16 (22 Apr 1915), 461.

34   "Emphatic Success of Bauer Compositions," *ML* 31/15 (13 Apr 1916), 461.

35   "Elsa Alves and Frank Hunter to Sing Bauer Compositions," *ML* 31/14 (6 Apr 1916), 430.

36   "Emphatic Success of Bauer Compositions," *ML* 31/15 (13 Apr 1916), 461.

37   Marion Bauer to A. P. Schmidt, 29 Sep 1916.

38   Marion Bauer in Chicago, *ML* 31/24 (15 June 1916), 839–840.

39   Marion Bauer to A. P. Schmidt, 6 Oct 1916.

40   "Worth-While American Composers," *The Musician* 8 (Aug 1926), 31.

41   Marion Bauer to A. P. Schmidt, 2 Aug 1916.

42   Marion Bauer to A. P. Schmidt, 24 Nov 1917.

43   Marion Bauer to A. P. Schmidt, 10 May 1918.

44   More information about this composition is found in Appendix 1. Complete information is found at marionbauer.org.

45   Marion Bauer to A. P. Schmidt, 16 July 1918.

46   *Oregonian,* "Music Vital Need," 20 July 1918, 5.

47   Emilie Frances Bauer, "Music in New York," *MLCG* 12/23 (6 Dec 1906), 6.

48   Emilie Frances Bauer, "Mahler as Symphony Conductor," *MLCG* 16/23 (3 Dec 1908), 9.

49   Emilie Frances Bauer, "The Mahler Symphony," *MLCG* 16/25 (17 Dec 1908), 9.

50   Emilie Frances Bauer, "Music in New York," *ML* 21/21 (25 May 1911), 9.

51   Marion Bauer to A. P. Schmidt, 9 April 1916. Marion did not specify which symphony she heard, but the date of her letter precisely correlates with a performance of his eighth symphony.

52   Emilie Frances Bauer, "Music in New York," *ML* 31/1 (20 Jan 1916), 72.

53   Emilie Frances Bauer, "Diaghileff Russian Ballet Makes First Appearance," *ML* 31/1 (20 Jan 1916), 76.

54   Emilie Frances Bauer, "Music in New York," *ML* 31/18 (4 May 1916), 554.

55   *NYT,* "Police are to Edit the Russian Ballet," 25 Jan 1916, 10.

56   *NYT,* "Russian Ballet Modified," 26 Jan 1916, 12.

57   *NYT,* "Russian Ballet Modified," 26 Jan 1916, 12.

58   "Many Receptions for Mrs. H. H. A. Beach," *ML* 29/11 (18 Mar 1915), 308.

59   Emilie Frances Bauer, "Music in New York," *ML* 29/9 (4 Mar 1915), 242.

60   "Wounds and Balm for the Women Composer," *ML* 30/5 (29 July 1915), 140.

CHAPTER 4

GIGGLES, LOVE, AND GRIEF

Emilie Frances Bauer, Composer

A s modernist composers grappled with attracting an audience, musical theatre and popular songs thrived. Surprisingly, Emilie Frances composed a handful of popular songs. Her earliest compositions for solo piano, in the 1880s, were mentioned in Chapter 1. Three decades elapsed, and then in 1916 she began publishing popular songs under the nom de plume Francisco di Nogero. It is possible, but unlikely, that during the interim years she published works under yet another, undiscovered, nom de plume.[1] Why "Francisco di Nogero"? She does not discuss the matter in her correspondence, but it makes sense that Francisco may stand for Frances, or perhaps San Francisco (her favorite city), and Nogero is Oregon spelled backwards. Frances of Oregon. It is curious that "Francisco" is sometimes misspelled "Francesco"––even in *The Musical Leader*––which may have been an inside joke for Emilie Frances, Marion, Flora, and their friends who were in cahoots with them, such as Florence French, who was the publisher and editor of *The Musical Leader*.[2]

One of Emilie Frances's songs, "My Love Is a Muleteer" ("El Arriero"; a muleteer is a person who drives mules), has an extraordinary history. The American Spanish Music Publishing Company first published it in 1916.

After the initial performances of the song, the sheet music immediately sold out.[3] A. P. Schmidt acquired the rights to the song and republished it in 1917. Although the music was attributed to Francisco di Nogero, the English lyrics were attributed to Emilie Frances. The song was a wild success with the public at the height of its popularity, when members of an audience would shout for "Muleteer" to be sung as an encore.[4] Certain singers were acknowledged for their particular affinity for the song: "[Mary Jordan's] skill in contrasts was fascinating as she sang with her well known diablerie and dash Francisco di Nogero's 'My love is a muleteer.'"[5] Music critics received the song coolly, even sarcastically, and speculated about the composer; for instance, A. W. Kramer wrote in *Musical America*, "Señor di Nogero (we believe he is a Spanish composer, perhaps a resident of San Sebastien)...has written a companion song to his 'My Love Is a Muleteer' called 'The Spanish Knight.' On the whole it is a rather better composition than the song just named, which, we hope, will not interfere with its being taken up by singers with the same avidity that they have shown in singing 'My Love Is a Muleteer.'"[6]

Emilie Frances had the piano accompaniment of the song orchestrated; she had someone else do it, which was a common practice. That version was recorded by the Columbia Graphophone Company, featuring Rosalie Miller, soprano. A second recording, featuring José Mardones singing the song in Spanish, sold extraordinarily well in Central and South America.[7] A voice and band version––sung by Delphine March and conducted by Edwin Franko Goldman––was performed with "tremendous" success to an audience of 25,000 people during a New York stadium concert.[8] Voice-quartet and duet arrangements of the song followed.[9]

Opening measures of "Muleteer."[10]

The Schmidt Company received inquiries about Francisco di Nogero, which were passed along to Emilie Frances. In response, Emilie Frances wrote a press release. Although she was asked to provide information about the composer, she ignores "him" almost entirely:

"My Love is a Muleteer" by Francisco di Nogero is a song that may be described as having had an extraordinary career. It was eagerly taken up and introduced by such artists as Julia Claussen, Sophie Braslau, Helen Stanley, Mary Jordan, Rosa Raisa and a very long and important list of others. None of these artists have dropped it, not only because it is a favorite with the singers, but when it is not found on the programs, they receive requests that they sing it as "encore" and so it goes its way dashingly. By means of the talking machine the Nardones records have made it equally familiar in South America and Latin countries where his discs are household idols and where it has been made known through Rosa Raisa's great success with the song to say naught of records made by Rosalie Miller and others.

Now it comes out of the air, literally speaking and has proven as successful a song for those who have sung for the Radio broadcasting all over the country. The composer has been literally deluged with letters from all parts of the country paraphrasing the old saying "I saw your ad in the paper" into "I heard your 'Muleteer' over the radio, and I tell you it came with a dash."[11]

Occasionally, Emilie Frances would write a review of a recital in which "Muleteer" was performed. In one such review, she wrote, "The dashing, vivacious melody converted Mme. [Helen] Stanley's whole audience into clamorous children who would have more at any cost, and the hubbub was only stilled when the singer gave the entire song again."[12] Emilie Frances's opinion about the artistic quality of her song is not known in so many words. However, in an editorial she wrote within a couple of years of "Muleteer's" publication, she does express a strong opinion about the place of such songs within the larger perspective of American art:

America has some composers who do not aspire to popularity, who write to express the best that is in them, and these are the works that should be considered as representative, not the "catchy," light, frothy music in which American composers are supreme. A warning may be sounded at this moment against catering to the popular taste which the publishers seem to be inviting. The ballad song with sentimental appeal which is intended for the entertainment of the boys in army life has its place; the strong rhythmic tune which sets all singing and time tapping has a very marked place and is dear to those in camps and to many who need recreation, but such music has small part in the development of American composition.... It would be impossible to believe that something really great could be written by one who seated himself as though in the limelight in front of a mirror to note what effect certain things would have upon the public. Arthur Foote, George W. Chadwick, Edward A. MacDowell, Mrs. H. H. A. Beach, Charles T. Griffes, Marion Bauer and a few such have written with never a thought of public or publisher.[13]

"My Love is a Muleteer" exemplifies "light, frothy music" and text:

My Love is a dashing muleteer / He comes thro' the rugged mountain passes; / He leaves a trail of love and fear, / Ohé for the broken-hearted lasses. / Ohé for the lads with cold steel blades, / They wait in vain for my Rodriguero / Who comes to dance in the evening shades, / With me to tread the gay Bolero. / Tra-la-la-la [etc.] / What will he bring to me my dear? / A scarlet band for my coal black tresses, / A throbbing heart in his manly breast, / Two loving arms filled with caresses. / I'll tread to the tune of the old guitar, / And the step of my dearest Rodriguero, / We'll dance in the ruddy evening glow / And we'll float away in the gay Bolero.

The rhythm of a bolero pervades the song. It is the sort of song that is a debacle in the hands of an amateur performer; its success is dependent upon a superb singer with dramatic flair to rescue it from being maudlin. Fortunately for Emilie Frances, a plethora of such artists performed it. Substantial royalties for the printed music, performance rights, and recordings provided a welcome financial cushion. One of the royalty checks was $275 ($3,500 in 2012 dollars),[14] which at that time paid several months rent. The lyrics of "Muleteer" are overtly sexual and yet they are the only part of the song to which Emilie Frances publicly attached her name. She was a sometimes prudish, unmarried woman who even took umbrage with dancing the tango,[15] yet she had an almost magical touch with innuendo.

Occasionally, *The Musical Leader* would subtly hint to the public about the identity of the true composer: "Of a musical family, [Marion] is the sister of another composer, Emilie Frances Bauer, the author of two of the greatest song successes of recent years, and journalist of distinction."[16] Clearly one of the greatest song successes is "Muleteer," but given that the song title is not specified, the author's identity is not overtly disclosed. Her secret was finally revealed in one of her obituaries.[17]

Amidst the frivolity, intrigue, and shenanigans surrounding "Muleteer," Emilie Frances composed a war song, "Our Flag in France," which she dedicated to "Our Boys." She had the music engraved, published it privately, and contributed all royalties to the American Ambulance Hospital in Paris. *The Musical Leader* announced its publication: "Miss Bauer is not making her debut as a composer, for she has to her credit a large number of songs which have been sung by noted artists, which have been published under a nom-de-plume."[18] However, her particular nom de plume was not stated, again preserving her anonymity. Also, giving her credit for a large number of songs was quite an exaggeration: she had composed no more than seven that we know of, and three of those were written much earlier, during her Walla Walla years. Schmidt later published four additional songs under the name Nogero, and Emilie Frances wrote the texts for three of them. "La Gitanina (From Roumanian Fields)" is, according to *The Musical Leader*, "a lengthy aria in which beauty of diction told the tragic story of devastated Rumanian fields."[19] The story originates with the

1907 Rumanian peasants' revolt, during which the army gunned down over 10,000 people. This music, with words also by Emilie Frances, is in striking contrast to "Muleteer": it is lengthier, less predictable, and much more serious. The Schmidt Company published the "Nogero" song "The Shadowy Garden" in 1921. One letter from Emilie Frances regarding this song is particularly amusing: "I can not imagine how it happened but a considerable number of 'The Shadowy Garden' was mislaid during 'housecleaning,' that worst period in a human being's existence."[20]

Among Emilie Frances's last known compositions are two songs from 1921: "The Lost Lagoon" and "Neither Spirit nor Bird." She called them "Indian lyrics."[21] Neither manuscript has been located. Judging from the title of the latter, that song's text is based on a popular Shoshone Indian love poem.[22] She approached Austin about publishing them: "I trust that you will like the fruit of my labors. Marion does and I always feel that to be the highest meed of praise so far as I am concerned."[23] However, the Schmidt Company did not publish any more of Emilie Frances's songs, either under her name or her pen name,[24] and as far as we know she did not compose after 1921.

Emilie Frances Bauer, ca. 1920.[25]

Charles T. Griffes

During the time when Emilie Frances briefly dove into composing again, Marion experienced her only known intimate connection with a man. One of Marion's students wrote, "Marion Bauer wore an engagement ring; the rumor I heard was that it was for an engagement to Charles Tomlinson Griffes. I don't know if there is any truth to that."[26] Today Charles T. Griffes (1884-1920) is remembered as one of the most important American composers of his generation, whose works *The Pleasure-Dome of Kubla Kahn, Clouds, The White Peacock*, and many others, are still performed regularly. Born in Elmira, New York, Griffes studied in Berlin in the early twentieth century, but was drawn most strongly to the French impressionist style. He taught at the Hackley School in Tarrytown, New York, and his works were just becoming more widely known when Marion met him.

Marion first heard Griffes's music in 1917 when one of Heffley's students played a work by him. Coincidentally, one week later, Rothwell told Marion that he had met Griffes was very impressed with one of his orchestral works. Rothwell mentioned Marion's compositions to Griffes, and Griffes said he would like to meet her. They quickly became close friends. Marion recounted, "Gradually we formed a musical society of two—he showed me his manuscripts and I showed him mine, and I received many constructive criticisms and suggestions from him."[27]

Marion and Griffes conversed about music, attended concerts together, and exchanged letters when one or the other was away.[28] Marion's many professional contacts were also beneficial for him. Three stand out: Eugene Heffley (to whom Marion introduced Griffes), the pianist Harold Bauer (1873–1951; no relation to Marion), and the Flonzaley Quartet. They all enthusiastically championed Griffes's music. The rumor that Marion and Griffes were lovers is easily explained: they were frequent, fond companions at social events. Edward Maisel, a Griffes biographer, writes, "What touched Griffes was [Marion's] spirit of fresh cheer, so much in contrast to his own tiredness and intermittent pessimism. She had hardly tried her wings yet, and her feeling of hope was almost contagious. She and her sister were also good fun. Once learning of Griffes's penchant for chocolate cake they baked one for dinner, only to learn that they had committed the unforgivable error of mixing a white interior when what he really favored was 'chocolate all through.' There was always welcome frivolity at the Bauers'."[29]

Griffes and Marion were not lovers. (The engagement ring Marion's student noticed was a family heirloom.)[30] Griffes was homosexual, and he very likely confided that fact to Marion when he knew he could trust her discretion. Donna Anderson, author of *Charles T. Griffes: A Life in Music*, interviewed Griffes's sister, Marguerite, and inquired about the nature of his relationship with Marion. In an email to the author, she writes,

> In a personal interview with Marguerite Griffes (his youngest sister) in San Francisco on 23 July 1969, she remarked that Griffes and Bauer were "very, very good friends." I asked Marguerite if Bauer had a little "crush" on Charles. She said, "I think she did." But Marguerite also said, "Afterwards [after Griffes's death], we never thought anything about it [at the time], but things she used to say, that she felt she knew him about as well as anybody." Then Marguerite brought up Babe Shoobert, also a close friend of Griffes, and Marguerite recalled, "I remember, I think in his diaries he spoke about that one night they [Griffes and Babe Shoobert] took a long walk and told each other things that they had never said before. So I had an idea that they *knew* about Charlie." [Griffes did write such an entry in his diary on 7 November 1914, "After the theater we walked home and had a very confidential talk. We told each other many things we hadn't told before."] The next thing Marguerite said was, "But I think, I always thought that Bauer thought she was about his chief friend." So, it is possible that the family also thought that Bauer knew about Charles. It is very hard to believe that Bauer did not

99

know that Griffes was homosexual, in spite of his innate private nature and discretion.[31]

Rumors about Marion and Griffes may also have been fueled by her remarkable change in appearance after she met him.

Marion Bauer, ca. 1916.[32]

Marion Bauer, ca. 1920.[33]

Donna Anderson's observations about Marion's change in appearance are helpful:

> Griffes might just have said to her, "Marion, you would look so nice with your hair cut this way, wearing this dress," etc. He did this with all the women in his family as well, and I have no doubt he didn't hesitate to "suggest" such things to his female friends. Even his sister-in-law... remarked about how well and carefully dressed Griffes himself always was.... Mary S. Broughton, Griffes's first piano teacher...made the same sort of suggestions to the young Griffes––how to dress, corrected his speech, table manners, etc. He took her suggestions gladly and probably thought others would take his with the same attitude.[34]

Shortly after Griffes met Marion, his music became widely acclaimed. The conductors Pierre Monteux, Leopold Stokowski, and Walter Damrosch all awaited scores and parts for Griffes's orchestral works, which were to premiere in 1919 and 1920 with, respectively, the Boston Symphony Orchestra, the Philadelphia Orchestra, and the New York Symphony Orchestra. Griffes worked feverishly during the summer of 1919 (when he was free from his teaching duties) preparing the manuscripts, during which time his health noticeably deteriorated from complications of influenza.[35] His last public appearance was at the premiere of his *The Pleasure-Dome of Kubla Khan,* which was performed by the Boston Symphony Orchestra. Only three weeks later, he was not well enough to attend the Philadelphia Orchestra's premieres of his four other works. Charles Griffes died on 8 April 1920 at the age of 35. After his death, Marion made a pilgrimage to his studio at the Hackley School and later assisted the Griffes family with sorting through his manuscripts. We do not have a first-hand account of Marion's emotions about Griffes's death. We do have a footnote in Edward Maisel's book that claims, "Marion Bauer...for much of the rest of her life wove a sometimes tearful myth of amorous connection with the composer. During the funeral and period of mourning for Griffes, she installed herself among the immediate family circle in a determined takeover capacity, almost (according to Griffes's mother) like an unacknowledged daughter-in-law asserting her rights."[36] To put it mildly, Maisel's depiction is unsympathetic and insensitive.

When Marion was counseling her young friend, the composer Ruth Crawford (1901–1953),[37] about intimate emotions, perhaps Marion was referring to her own feelings for Griffes when she said: "Sublimation–you are right, you can sublimate. I had a beautiful friend who taught me that."[38] Ruth Crawford said, about Marion, "She has suffered. She has loved and has suffered, and she is radiant." Rumors and speculation aside, Charles Griffes was Marion's first and only intimate male acquaintance, so far as we know. She was devoted. Was the devotion that of admiration for his musical genius? Was it love? It was probably both.

We see Griffes's influence in Marion's *Three Impressions* for solo piano, which were composed shortly after she met him. Griffes's *Roman Sketches* (1916) is a suite of four pieces, each of which is preceded by a poem by William Sharp. Marion's *Three Impressions* (1917) is a suite of three pieces, each of which is preceded by a poem by John Gould Fletcher. The *Roman Sketches* exhibit many impressionist characteristics, although Griffes's style is personal and unique; so too with Marion's *Three Impressions*. More technical skill is required here than in any of her earlier piano works. The first movement, "The Tide," is an exquisite, watery portrayal of the poem: "The tide makes music / At the foot of the beach; / The waves sing together." "Druids," in ternary form (A-B-A), has a moody and dark opening and closing, and an insistent low-E pedal point; the middle section brightens the otherwise brooding movement. In the last movement, "Vision," Marion indicates on the sheet music that the opening theme is to be played softly and "tenderly and with longing." That theme returns periodically, but in different registers of the piano, and with engaging variation, all of which is occasionally interrupted by *forte* flourishes.[39]

A. Walter Kramer, a critic for *Musical America*, wrote:

> Her "Druids," which is now before us, is one of "Three
> Impressions for the Pianoforte, Op. 10." The other two,
> "The Tide" and "Vision," have not yet been received, but

if they are anything like "Druids" (and we believe they are) Miss Bauer will have to put to her credit one of the finest sets of piano pieces that we know by a contemporary composer.

Miss Bauer is to-day one of our most richly gifted creative women and nowhere has she shown it more convincingly than in her "Druids." It is a slow movement, a real impression, deeply poetic, finely suggestive and, above all, sincere and to the point. There is themal development here; there is harmonic subtlety and the manner in which the theme is each time transformed by means of a harmonic alteration is individual and full of personality. The reiterated low bass E throughout the piece from time to time acts almost like an organ point interrupted by the poetic message.... It is, in short, an exceptional composition for piano, one that Miss Bauer must be proud of.[40]

Opening of "Druids." The pedal point on E is evident through this section. At times the pedal point is a member of the chord above it, and at other times it is dissonant. Note the pattern created in the first two measures, which is then repeated (with alterations) again and again, rising in both pitch and dynamics.[41]

Shortly thereafter, Kramer reviewed the other two movements:

> We found "Druids" a very unusual piece, a composition that would command respect anywhere where musical art is appreciated.

"The Tide" is also a remarkable bit of writing. To the lover of richly colored modern music it will make an immediate appeal. "Vision," with its shifting harmonies and rhythms, pleases us even more. We are almost inclined to record that it is the best of the set. Miss Bauer goes deep into the problem of latter-day harmony in this work, experimenting in things that our forefathers forbade their composition pupils even to dream, much less write. The design is engaging, the architecture solidly handled and thematically, too, the piece is strong and convincing.... They belong among the very best contemporary piano music.[42]

Rudolph Ganz (1877–1972), pianist and director of the St. Louis Symphony from 1921 to 1927, spoke of both Marion's and Griffes's music, "Charles T. Griffes' new piano sonata...is free from all foreign influences. He is going his own way and so is Marion Bauer in her three new piano pieces [*Three Impressions*]. These two reach out for new problems and don't lean upon an Indian or negro theme in order to make the people believe they are American. What is more, these pieces are very accessible to advanced students and should be very successful."[43]

Although Griffes himself, and his music, may have inspired Marion's *Three Impressions*, the suite is dedicated to her piano teacher, Eugene Heffley. Marion commented, "[They] seem so much more my own than many other things I have done."[44]

The MacDowell Colony

During the summer of 1919, Marion spent her first summer at the MacDowell Colony in Peterborough, New Hampshire. The Colony was founded in 1907 around Edward MacDowell's (1860–1908) summer home. It was later expanded, partially financed, and managed by his widow, Marian MacDowell (1857–1956), as a working haven for composers, writers, visual artists, film makers, and architects.[45] The Colony was Marion's refuge during numerous subsequent summers. Marion reflected:

> Surrounded by beauties of nature and material comforts, with absolute freedom from responsibility, at an expense so small that one could not possibly live in any city so economically, [the artist] works in peace. He may have solitude when he likes and companionship when he has time, for to be undisturbed at work is the supreme privilege of the colony.

> That we are not all working in the same branch is a delightful fact, for there is the broadening influence of meeting people who not caring at all for music, yet bring you a new point of view and new experience from other arts, as many of the colonists are important in their respective fields; and yet the spirit underlying the different lines of work makes one realize that these branches after all have one gigantic trunk in common and are individual mediums for the same creative urge....

> My own studio was unique. Mrs. MacDowell turned the loft of her barn into a work room and supplied me with a piano, and I had a wonderful view of rolling hills and peaceful New England farms with Mount Monadnock in the distance.[46]

During her first summer there, Marion composed three songs on texts by her fellow colonist, Katherine Adams: "Gold of the Day and Night," "Thoughts," and "The Driftwood Fire." They are rather tame songs harmonically and technically, perhaps accounting for the Schmidt Company publishing them. She also composed "My Faun," with a text by Oscar Wilde (who was one of Griffes's favorite poets) that same summer. Wilde's poetry was very different from Katherine Adams's, and Marion's music changed as well. She composed the song for a professional-level singer, judging by the range and some unusual and large leaps. She dedicated it to Mary Jordan, who premiered the work in Aeolian Hall in the fall of 1919.[47] The piano opens the song with a haunting and memorable motive that returns periodically. The motive is slightly reminiscent of the opening of Charles Griffes's *White Peacock* (1915–1916), which Marion, no doubt, had thoroughly absorbed, and also of Debussy's opening of *Prélude à l'après-midi d'un faune.* Perhaps both Marion and Griffes were paying tribute to that landmark composition. Marion's title certainly suggests that she was doing so. The sudden changes of mood in the song are appealing. The holograph of "My Faun" is a rough draft with numerous emendations, arrows, and crossouts. Since the song was not published during Marion's lifetime, a performer today would have to conjecture occasionally as to what some of the holograph markings mean.

Holograph of "My Faun," page one.[48]

While at the MacDowell Colony, Marion was also working on her first book, *How Music Grew*, and on an article that was published in *The Musical Quarterly* a few months later, "Natural Law: Its Influence on Modern Music." In the article she outlined her philosophical view of modern sounds, nature, and the modern listener. Marion wrote (perhaps "hoped" is also apt):

> We are children of the age which produced us, and this particular period is one of great complexities not the least of which is modern harmony. But the ear is tremendously elastic in its adjusting powers, and a public is soon educated, or at least accustoms itself rapidly to new combinations of tone.

> There *is* an inherent power in music of which we have touched only the outer rim, and as man's perceptions become more highly sensitized, more of the "Music of the Spheres" will be disclosed to us, and the music of the future may bear much the same relation to what we have already wrested from Nature, as wireless telegraphy bears to our first crude experiments with poles and wires.[49]

Following Griffes's death in 1920, Marion spent her second summer at the MacDowell Colony. There she composed her set of solo piano pieces, *From the New Hampshire Woods*, which was inspired by the beauty of nature that surrounded her there. Each of the three movements is preceded by a poem. The first movement, "White Birches," is a good piece that, although not overly technically demanding, needs a pianist's expert judgment to know which lines should be emphasized; without such artistry the piece could sound commonplace. "Indian Pipes" is a musical depiction of a plant with a drooping flower. Here, a pianist's attention to tempo changes and color are critical to the success of the movement, which suffers a little from too much emphasis on the middle register of the piano. "Pine-Trees" is arguably the best of the three movements. The captivating main theme is brought back in various guises, and the 5/4 time signature allows for mercurial melodic and harmonic motion.[50]

Pine-Trees

Pine-trees on the dark-strewn hillside
Hear the dreams the river blows them.
Pine-trees, standing quiet there and listening,
You have heard the dreams of God.

M. Hardwicke Nevin

Marion Bauer. Op. 12, No. 3

Opening of "Pine-Trees." Note the descending chromatic motion in an inner voice, which is present in several Bauer works.[51]

Marion sent *From the New Hampshire Woods* to Austin. Although he kept the score for some time, he was not planning to publish it in the near future. When Oscar Sonneck (1873–1928), director of publications at the G. Schirmer Company, heard a performance and wanted to publish it, Marion politely asked permission of Austin, because simultaneously submitting a composition to more than one publisher was considered underhanded, if not unethical.[52] Austin agreed to relinquish it, and shortly thereafter it was published and received very positive reviews in *The Musical Observer*[53] and *Musical America*.[54]

Regarding her *Sonata for Violin and Piano in G Minor*, which at this point she had worked on during two summers at the Colony, she wrote a bubbly letter to Austin: "I am working on my violin sonata and hope to have it ready by fall [1920] to show to anyone who wants to see it. Do you? Of course it is the most pretentious thing I have ever attempted, but I am enthusiastic about the creative part of the work––It has been great fun."[55] Eighteen months later, the sonata was completed.

Around the same time, Erminie Kahn interviewed Marion for an article about her recent compositions that provides insight into how some members of the musical community were viewing Marion's style. Marion takes umbrage, both at being labeled an "intellectual composer," and at the idea that a composer who deeply studies the music of others, and the theoretical foundations of music, might relinquish creativity:

> Miss Bauer has been called an intellectual composer, which does not altogether please her. She feels that there is sometimes a reproach in the word "intellectual." She is a scholarly musician and has studied seriously in America and in Europe with the best masters and, having a keen and observing mind, has evolved a musical individuality. This may be why she is considered "intellectual." It is well known that whatever she writes is done with a knowledge of the scientific laws of music as well as with a poetic interpretation of mood. "I do not believe that everyone is fitted to be a composer," said Miss Bauer, "but, given a talent, there comes the proposition of development. I deny that any one can do too much studying; it never robs one of spontaneity where there is spontaneity originally, and completeness of expression can only come with freedom in technical equipment."[56]

Was one of Schmidt's objections to Marion's works their intellectual character? If he equated modernism with intellectualism, then perhaps so. Without his half of the correspondence, this remains speculative. Other publishers now accepted songs that Schmidt had rejected: "Night in the Woods," "Roses Breathe in the Night," and "Epitaph of a Butterfly." Marion wrote to Austin, "There are three new songs out––two Schirmer and one Ditson. Would it interest you to see what songs that you turned down look like in print?"[57] Perhaps she regretted the tone of her statement when two weeks later she learned of the death of Arthur P. Schmidt on 5 May 1921. Schmidt's death was the culmination of several years of tragedies for the Bauer sisters. Death, premature and otherwise, haunted them from 1913–1920.

Julia H. Bauer Dies

Unlike Marion's father, Jacques, Marion's mother, Julia, lived to see her youngest child enjoy her early career triumphs. In 1913, at the age of seventy, she was recently retired in Portland, Oregon. Emilie Frances, Marion, and their sister Flora all traveled there by train to be with their mother during her last days.[58] Nearly twenty-three years had elapsed since Jacques's death. Still, Julia's burial in the Beth Israel Cemetery in Portland, rather than beside her husband in Walla Walla, seems odd. Whether she or her children made that decision is unknown. A friend of Julia's memorialized her in the *Oregonian*:

> Those who were fortunate enough to meet her socially or in literary study will ever remember the enthusiasm with which she advanced her own views or theories or gently indicated a mistaken judgment. Hers was a character moulded in a mind which grew broader and stronger as the years rolled by. This may account for the liberal views she religiously entertained. While tutored and trained in the old Jewish school and home, her convictions carried her out in the arena where the divine spirit reckons not with creed, but calls for the deeds that can benefit all mankind....
>
> When left a widow with the care of her young children 22 years ago, she did not despair, but energetically devoted herself to their best education, never commanding but always urging and consulting their wishes and inclination for life's calling. How happy in her just and motherly pride when, once a year at this season, she gathered around her family hearthstone those whom she had fitted for the

battles of life and listened to proud achievements and hopes.[59]

Drawing too many conclusions about Julia's connection with her children based only on this idealized tribute would risk inaccuracy, but it's worth noting that, in this reminiscence, Julia's attributes as a scholar, an intellectual, and a teacher, are conjoined with her relationships to her children. No doubt she did "devote herself to their best education," and that they all heartily benefitted, but we're left to wonder how much warmth her children experienced from her.

Eighteen months after Julia's death, Marion wrote, "My mother was one of the noblest women who has ever lived."[60] Twenty years later Marion wrote, "My mother was a linguist and a scholar who spent most of her life with her books."[61] She distanced herself from her mother in both statements, first through idealizing her as "noble," and second through "scholarly" criticism. That Emilie Frances, Marion, and Flora had all moved 3,000 miles away from Julia amplifies the ambiguity of the parental bond. The New York-based sisters did travel across the country each year to spend time with their mother, brother Cecil, and fourth sister Minnie, all of whom resided in Portland. Whatever faults Julia may or may not have had, it is obvious that she modeled modern womanhood for her daughters. Thanks to her they saw education as a path to self-sufficiency, independence, and creativity. They did not think that womanhood was a lesser condition, only a different condition. They embraced the notion of woman as breadwinner and the responsibilities and freedoms represented therein. The Bauer women were champions of modernism, professionalism, and feminism, not so much as political activists, but by the way they conducted their lives and careers.

Minnie, who had resided with Julia up to this time, now moved to New York to live with her sisters. Minnie was said to be a "partial cripple" as the result of having suffered from scarlet fever as a child.[62] However, scarlet fever in itself is not a crippling disease.[63] It is more likely that Minnie was mildly intellectually challenged: her signature on legal documents is very child-like, although the Federal Census of 1900 indicates Minnie could read and write. If she were intellectually challenged, social stigma at the time may have compelled the family to use a medical excuse for her condition.[64] After Julia's death, Minnie was uprooted from the familiar surroundings of Portland, where Cecil and his wife continued to live, possibly because of signs of mental illness in Cecil's wife. The absence of personal Bauer family correspondence renders Minnie's story frustratingly spare. Her condition, and what the sisters' duties were in regard to her, are largely unknown.

At the time of Julia's death, Cecil was a successful lawyer with his own firm, Bauer and Greene. He was also a Colonel and Judge Advocate General in the Oregon National Guard. His wife, Rose Bloch Bauer, was a highly regarded soprano and vocal teacher who performed occasionally in New York, where she presented Marion's songs.[65] Both Cecil and Rose were engaged in philanthropic activities, including "promoting charitable enterprises and movements designed to assist Jewish peoples."[66] Cecil was a founding member of the Tualatin Golf Club, which allowed Jewish members, unlike the other golf clubs in Portland.[67]

A year after Julia's death, Flora (now forty-two years old) married R. Alexander Bernstein.[68] The ceremony took place in the Bauer sisters' apartment in New York City. After their marriage, Flora and her husband took an apartment within a block or two of Marion, Emilie Frances, and Minnie. Is there significance in the fact that Marion was in Europe during this wedding, the only wedding among the Bauer sisters? Or that the wedding took place a year after Julia's death? Or that Julia never witnessed the marriage of any of her daughters? We don't know. It is tempting to speculate that Julia may have had some objection to the marriage. That said, waiting for the wedding until one year had elapsed after Julia's death was in line with mourning etiquette at that time. Given that only one of the four sisters did marry, it seems clear that they likely did not have a traditional view of marriage as a social necessity. Marion's absence at the wedding is easier to understand: she taught piano and theory lessons during the music season, which allowed only the summer for extensive study abroad.

Grief Upon Grief

Around the time of Flora's wedding, Cecil's wife, Rose, suffered a "nervous breakdown." Then a year later an automobile in which she was riding struck a child, and she never recovered from the shock. She died in 1915 at the age of forty-two, after having been bedridden for three months.[69] Then Cecil died suddenly in 1917 at the age of forty-seven.[70] The only known personal description of him is in an obituary: "He was a quiet, unassuming gentleman, who, in an unostentatious, self-sacrificing way, was always doing a world of good. Of an artistic, discriminating temperament, he shunned hullabaloo, noise and pretense. His philanthropic endeavor was broader than any religion or race. Never was he a slacker in any civic or humanitarian duty."[71] The four sisters traveled from New York City to Portland to bury their beloved brother. Only one letter, written by Marion to Schmidt shortly after Cecil's death, reveals the depth of her mourning at that time, "The suddenness of my brother's death has been a shock that we can't get over quickly. I feel often too tired to exert myself to any extent, but I hope soon to be myself again.... I had hoped that I could make a visit to Boston when my brother came East to spend the holidays but of course he did not have that chance to be with us once more."[72]

Just over two years later, in April 1920, Marion's close friend Charles Griffes died at the age of thirty-five. Then, a few months after Griffes's death, Minnie was killed. A memorial appeared in *The Musical Leader*. From it we can see that Minnie was not hidden from the Bauer sisters' friends and colleagues:

> One of the saddest occurrences recently was the death of Minnie Bauer, sister of Emilie Frances Bauer of The Musical Leader. Miss Minnie Bauer was struck by an automobile Monday afternoon, Aug. 23 [1920], and died that evening. She was buried on Thursday, her funeral being attended by a large number of personal friends. This gentle, kindly woman, who was the "home body" of the Bauer family and who was greatly beloved, had lived the greater part of her life in Portland, Ore., where

her people had settled many years ago. Upon the death of her mother (one of the most brilliant scholars the West has ever known), she took up her residence with her sisters, Emilie Frances Bauer, Flora Bauer Bernstein (well known to the musical profession) and Marion Bauer, the composer. Minnie Bauer's death will be a severe loss to those who knew the character and disposition of one of nature's noble-women.[73]

During these several years of enduring so many deaths, the close physical proximity of the sisters meant no letters passed among them that would help now to recreate a more empathetic, personal, and detailed perspective. Surely it seems to be a period of unrelenting and unimaginable grief.

Financial Matters

During these years of witnessing the decimation of their family, the Bauer sisters had to attend to the legal and financial ramifications of the deaths. Julia's instructions in her Last Will and Testament were "share and share alike," with the notable exceptions being that she gave her library and her diamond engagement ring to Emilie Frances.[74] Emilie Frances was trustee of Julia's estate. She and her siblings immediately put Julia's assets in a trust "for the support, nurture, comfort and care of…Minnie Bauer."[75]

Four years later, Cecil left an estate valued at $50,000 (about $885,000 in 2012), plus life insurance policies.[76] Minnie's financial care was spelled out, "I hereby request and direct my sisters Emilie Frances Bauer, Flora Bernstein and Marion E. Bauer, or the survivors of them, who may have the care of my sister Minnie Bauer, to invest the proceeds of life insurance policies on my life, and the proceeds from the sale of any property…to which said Minnie Bauer shall be entitled…so that there shall always be a definite and assured income therefrom to suitably care for my said sister Minnie Bauer."[77] The remainder of the estate was shared equally among the sisters. Each, then, inherited a significant sum.[78]

At the time of Minnie's death in 1920, her considerable inheritances from both Julia and Cecil, which had been invested and managed by Emilie Frances, were now passed on to the three remaining sisters. Although legal documents do not spell out precisely what they inherited, a conservative estimate would be $300,000 for each sister (in 2012 dollars).[79]

One final point regarding Marion's significant inheritance is that her comments about struggling financially during the ensuing two decades are puzzling. Judging from the relative value of Marion's inheritance in 1920, compared with the value of her estate at the time of her death in 1955, it appears that she probably chose not to touch much of her nest egg, even during the Great Depression. She seems to have remained financially very secure.[80]

---

[1]   She may have also used the *nom de plume* "E. Manolito," but that has not been confirmed.

[2]   Emilie Frances Bauer to H. R. Austin, 15 Apr 1922, A. P. Schmidt Co. Archives, business papers/correspondence/box 7, Library of Congress, Washington, DC.

[3]   "Arthur P. Schmidt Announces Novelties," *ML* 32/25 (21 Dec 1916), 684.

[4]   "Helen Stanley's Success at Stadium," *ML* 38/5 (31 July 1919), 100.

[5]   "Mary Jordan Thrills Thousands," *ML* 40/1 (1 July 1920), 7.

[6]   A. W. K, [A. Walter Kramer], "New Music—Vocal and Instrumental," *MA* 27/23 (6 Apr 1918): 40.

[7]   Details about these two recordings are found in Appendix 3.

[8]   Emilie Frances Bauer to H. R. Austin, 29 July 1920.

[9]   Emilie Frances Bauer to H. R. Austin, 24 July 1922.

[10]   More information about this composition is found in Appendix 2. Complete information is found at marionbauer.org.

[11]   Emilie Frances Bauer, "A Song With Extraordinary Career," [press release regarding "My Love Is a Muleteer,"] A. P. Schmidt Co. Archives, business papers/correspondence/box 7, Library of Congress, Washington, DC.

[12]   "Mme. Stanley's Brilliant Recital," *ML* 34/25 (20 Dec 1917), 650.

[13]   Emilie Frances Bauer, "Music in New York," *ML* 36/1 (4 July 1918), 3.

[14]   Emilie Frances Bauer to H. R. Austin, 11 May 1921.

[15]   Emilie Frances Bauer, "Music in New York," *ML* 27/2 (8 Jan 1914), 43.

[16]   "An American Composer Who Has Won Signal Honors," *ML* 38/4 (24 July 1919), 81.

[17]   "Emilie Frances Bauer Dies in New York," *Musical Digest* 9/22 (16 Mar 1926), 1.

18 "Song Royalties for the Wounded," *ML* 34/4 (26 July 1917), 84.

19 "Mary Jordan Delights Audience in Recital Hall," *ML* 38/23 (4 Dec 1919), 543.

20 Emilie Frances Bauer to H. R. Austin, 20 Sep 1921.

21 Emilie Frances Bauer to H. R. Austin, 15 Aug 1921.

22 Mary Austin, translator, "Neither Spirit nor Bird," *Poetry* 9/5 (Feb 1917): 239.

23 Emilie Frances Bauer to H. R. Austin, 15 Aug 1921.

24 H. R. Austin to Emilie Frances Bauer, 14 Feb 1924.

25 *ML*, 39/23 (3 June 1920), 594.

26 William Shank, letter to author, 18 July 2006.

27 Marion Bauer, "Charles T. Griffes as I Remember Him," *MQ* 29/3 (July 1943): 365–366.

28 Ibid., 369 and 372.

29 Edward Maisel, *Charles T Griffes* (New York: Da Capo Press, 1972), 189–190.

30 A picture of Marion wearing the ring was sent to the daughter of the person to whom the ring was bequeathed. She confirmed that it was Julia's engagement ring.

31 Donna Anderson, email correspondence with author, 8 Dec 2006. Brackets are Anderson's.

32 *ML* 31/24 (15 June 1916), 839.

33 *ML* 44/6 (10 Aug 1922), 121.

34 Donna Anderson, email correspondence with author, 8 Dec 2006.

35 Donna Anderson, *Charles T. Griffes: A Life in Music* (DC and London: Smithsonian Institution Press, 1993), 169.

36 Maisel, 382.

37 Ruth Crawford later married Charles Seeger, and became Ruth Crawford Seeger.

38 Judith Tick, *Ruth Crawford Seeger: A Composer's Search for American Music.* (New York: Oxford University Press, 1997), 97 and 107.

39 A recording of *Three Impressions* by the pianist Stephen Beus is available. See Appendix 3 for details.

40 A. W. K. [A. Walter Kramer], "New Music––Vocal and Instrumental," *MA* 27/23 (6 Apr 1918): 40.

41 More information about this composition is found in Appendix 1. Complete information is found at marionbauer.org.

42 A. W. K. [A. Walter Kramer], "New Music––Vocal and Instrumental," *MA* 26/5 (1 June 1918): 40.

43 "A Chat with Rudolph Ganz," *MC* 76/17 (25 Apr 1918), 10.

44 Marion Bauer to A. P. Schmidt, 31 Mar 1918.

45 Arnold Schwab and Charles Macy, "MacDowell Colony," *Grove Music Online*, ed. L. Macy. http://www.grovemusic.com (accessed 2 Aug 2006).

46 "MacDowell Spirit Inspires Work in Peterboro Colony," *ML* 38/10 (4 Sep 1919), 227.

[47]   Interestingly, on Gertrude Wieder's recital eleven years later, in Dec 1930, "Faun Song" was "introduced...from manuscript," after which Marion orchestrated "Faun Song" for alto and orchestra. It is highly likely that "My Faun," "The Faun," and "Faun Song" are all essentially the same piece, and that Marion had not decided yet which title she preferred.

[48]   More information about this composition is found in Appendix 1. Complete information is found at marionbauer.org.

[49]   Marion Bauer, "Natural Law: Its Influence on Modern Music," *MQ* 6/4 (Oct 1920): 473, 476.

[50]   A recording of "Pine-Trees" by the pianist Stephen Beus is available. See Appendix 3 for details.

[51]   More information about this composition is found in Appendix 1. Complete information is found at marionbauer.org.

[52]   Marion Bauer to H. R. Austin, 14 Nov 1921.

[53]   "New Music in Print," *Musical Observer* 22/5 (May 1923), 48.

[54]   Sydney Dalton, "New Music—Vocal and Instrumental," *MA* 37/21 (17 Mar 1923): 10.

[55]   Marion Bauer to H. R. Austin, 21 July 1920.

[56]   Erminie Kahn, "The Aims of Marion Bauer, Expression of All Moods in Music Sought by Composer Almost Unique in Writing for Piano—Her Scholarly Musicianship," *ML* 39/23 (3 June 1920), 550.

[57]   Marion Bauer to H. R. Austin, 19 Apr 1921.

[58]   "Noted Linguist Dead at Age of 70 Years." Newspaper clipping of unknown origin. Nellie Day scrapbook. (Walla Walla, WA: Whitman College archives, Bauer folder), [n.d., presumed to be July 1913].

[59]   A Friend [pseud.], "Tribute Paid to Life Devoted to Education," *Oregonian*, July 20 July 1913: 5.

[60]   Marion Bauer to A. P. Schmidt, 20 Jan 1915.

[61]   Ewen, *Composers of Today*, 15.

[62]   *Oregonian*, "Miss Minnie Bauer Dies," 27 Aug 1920, 6.

[63]   According to the physician, RA Johnson, perhaps rheumatic fever complicated a streptococcal infection, which is the cause of scarlet fever.

[64]   "Death of Mme. Julia Bauer," *ML* 26/5 (31 July 1913), 128. This obituary for Julia contains the only contradictory statement regarding Minnie's condition, wherein Flora and Minnie are characterized as "accomplished women."

[65]   "Rose Bloch Bauer Sings in New York," *ML* 27/11 (12 Mar 1914), 375.

[66]   *Portland Evening Telegram*, "Cecil Bauer Dies in Tacoma Hotel," 10 Dec 1917: 1.

[67]   Anne LeVant Prahl, Curator of the Oregon Jewish Museum, email to author, 13 March 2008.

[68]   *NYT*, "Married," 12 July 1914, C5. R. Alexander Bernstein's family had emigrated from London when he was a boy. At the turn of the century, he was

an art dealer in Portland, then later worked for Fairchild Publications in New York. Whether he knew Flora in Portland before he took up residence in New York is unknown, but highly likely because the Bauers and Bernsteins attended the same synagogue there.

[69] *Morning Oregonian*, "Rose Bloch Bauer Dies at Midnight," 14 June 1915, 1.

[70] *Portland Evening Telegram*, "Cecil H. Bauer Dies in Tacoma Hotel," 10 Dec 1917: 1. His obituaries stated he died of a heart attack, but his death certificate indicated he died of pancreatitis. According to the physician, RA Johnson, given the family history, he may have suffered from an infarct of the pancreas.

[71] "Cecil H. Bauer," *Oregon Voter* 11/11 (15 Dec 1917): 349.

[72] Marion Bauer to A. P. Schmidt, 18 Feb 1918.

[73] "Death of Minnie Bauer," *ML* 40/10 (2 Sep 1920), 228.

[74] Julia H. Bauer, will dated 30 August 1890, probate 15090, Circuit Court of the State of Oregon for the County of Multnomah, Portland, OR.

[75] Julia H. Bauer, will dated 30 August 1890, probate 15090, Exhibit A, Circuit Court of the State of Oregon for the County of Multnomah, Portland, OR.

[76] *Morning Oregonian*, "$50,000 Estate is Left," 21 Dec. 1917, 15; *Portland Telegram*, "Lawyer Leaves $5000 for Wife's Memorial," 20 Dec 1917, 1.

[77] Cecil H. Bauer, will dated 19 August 1914, probate 15030, County of Multnomah, Portland, OR.

[78] This statement is made with the assumption that newspaper articles declaring the dollar value of his estate were correct.

[79] The two estates combined are estimated to be worth about $1,000,000 (in 2012 dollars). We do not know how much of the money set aside for the care of Minnie had to be spent; given that she lived with family throughout her life, it seems most likely that the survivors of Minnie inherited a considerable amount of money.

[80] It is possible that Marion invested her inheritances in such a way that the money was not liquid. Another possibility is that she was not comfortable with anyone outside of her immediate family knowing about her financial affairs, so she may have cultivated the public perception that she lived solely on her income as a music teacher and composer. In either case, the value of her estate at the time of her death strongly suggests that a significant part of her estate was from her inheritances; neither her salary for teaching, nor her royalties from her published music, would generate that much money.

CHAPTER 5

CONTINENTAL DIVIDE

American Music Guild

Marion was one of the founding members of the American Music Guild (AMG) in 1921: "I was the only woman member of the American Music Guild, [which was] formulated...with the idea of playing and criticizing each other's music as well as giving hearing to new compositions. And believe me, they really ripped my music apart, and yet it was very helpful, for criticism never hurt anyone, least of all a sincere artist."[1]

The AMG presented two inaugural concerts in 1922 which included Marion's *Sonata for Violin and Piano in G Minor*. It was performed by Albert Stoessel (1894–1943), a violinist, composer, and conductor, and by the composer and pianist, Louis Gruenberg (1884–1964).[2] Marion's new sonata impressed a *Musical America* critic: "This sonata is one of the most distinguished products of our American composers––and it is the work of a woman! Miss Bauer's sonata, like her songs, reflects a lofty musical spirit, directed by a well-organized technique.... Altogether, Miss Bauer's sonata is a distinguished accomplishment, a composition that enriches our literature."[3]

Soon after the performance, Marion responded to Austin's lack of interest in publishing the work: "I was disappointed that you seemed disinclined to consider the Violin Sonata for future publication. I realize the expense of such an undertaking, but I also realize that a composer is not taken very seriously until he or she has shown the ability to produce a work of larger scope than song or piano composition."[4] A few months after its premiere performance, at a gathering to honor Amy Beach, the sonata was performed again, and the audience reacted so favorably that the last movement was repeated.[5] Sadly, the music has not been found.[6]

Six Preludes

When Austin unexpectedly sent Marion a $200 cash advance in 1922 (about $2,700 in 2012), it was probably for her *Six Preludes* for piano, which were in the final stages of editing. The magnitude of the advance suggests a generous response to Marion's comments about her financial circumstances: "Your letter reached me yesterday morning and I am quite at a loss of words to tell you how deeply I appreciate your kindness. The check has made things so much easier for me materially, but it did something much finer, because it showed me how genuinely the friendship started by Mr. Schmidt is being carried on."[7] Her comment about the advance affecting her "materially" supports the conjecture that she was adamant about preserving her inheritances.

Marion rejected the title *Six Modern Preludes*, on the grounds that "what is modern in 1922 will probably be quite conventional in 1940."[8] If only a few of Marion's works could be in mainstream literature today, the *Six Preludes* should be among them. They are beautifully crafted, each with its own mood, and together they form a cohesive yet varied group. Although the key of each prelude is announced in its title, those key centers serve only as focal points, around which triads and chromaticism freely interact. She rarely opens a prelude with a clear-cut key, but instead winds her way to the key center toward the end.

Although the first prelude is for the left hand only, it has a rich sound. It is one of the quieter and slower preludes, with a wistful and twisting melody, accompanied by offbeats in the lower register of the piano. Toward the end, she sets up the listener for what might be a typical ending on a D major triad, then she quietly but insistently sounds a dissonant pedal point. The effect is magical. It is dedicated to the composer-pianist Amy Beach, who performed it on several occasions. Paul Wittgenstein, the famed pianist who lost his right arm during warfare, often performed it. Percy Grainger, who also was a fan of the first prelude, said, "This charming lyric, so rich in dynamic shadings, seems to run the gamut of the best dreamily emotional possibilities of the left hand, plus a cunning use of the sustaining (middle) pedal."[9] The second prelude, in A minor, is a little faster, with similar harmonic sounds. Here Marion introduces a brief melody, which is subsequently varied with melodic and harmonic surprises. An astute listener will hear the two hands in conversation: the right hand plays a three or four note motive, which the left hand immediately imitates or turns upside down. It is dedicated to the acclaimed pianist Victor Wittgenstein (no relation to Paul Wittgenstein). Ernest Hutcheson, a renowned Australian pianist, is the dedicatee of the next prelude. Its energy, virtuosity, sparkle, and chromatic surprises create an irresistible one-minute gem.

Opening of the third prelude.[10]

The fourth prelude, in F-sharp major, is the most mercurial of the set. It begins with a carefree, cheerful rhythm that has an unpredictable pulse because the time-signature changes frequently, from 5/4 to 7/4 to 6/4. Then the majestic middle section switches the emphasis to chords and melody (somewhat reminiscent of Rimsky-Korsakov's "Great Gate of Kiev"), followed by a development of the melody, but now with an impressionistic, whole tone accompaniment. A return to the rhythmic vitality of the beginning rounds it out. It is dedicated to E. Robert Schmitz, who performed it frequently in America and Europe. The fifth prelude is quiet and reflective, and the most pervasively impressionistic in its melody and harmony. It is dedicated to the American pianist Harold Morris.[11] The last prelude, which is to be played "exuberantly, passionately," sounds inspired by Chopin's "Revolutionary Etude." It is a stormy, energetic, and riveting finale to the group of six.[12]

Richard Aldrich, a music critic for *The New York Times,* commented about some of the preludes: "Miss Bauer's three preludes develop widely different moods by frequent and incisive strokes in a strongly pianistic idiom."[13] *The Musical Leader* quoted a review that had appeared in the *Evening Sun*: "Miss Bauer's preludes…were enlivening, stirring; they leaped with verve and expert assurance."[14] An anonymous critic commented, "They showed a virility seldom heard in the compositions by women."[15]

Around the same time that she composed *Six Preludes,* Marion also composed *Three Preludettes* for piano. Austin declined to publish them, to which Marion responded, "I'm sorry you did not like the little Preludes––it is the kind of stuff I look for, for studies for my pupils. I suppose I am 'high brow' even in my teaching––what an awful calamity to be born so and to be unable to overcome it!"[16] (Several of Marion's pedagogical works are much more musically sophisticated than typical teaching repertoire.) G. Schirmer did publish them the next year, in 1923. That year was pivotal for Marion: she moved to Paris for an extended period of studying and composing.

Marion in Paris

"I am dazed these days at the prospect of leaving my family and tearing myself up by the roots but I know once I am at work I shall be happy and find satisfaction in the leisure, and, I hope, the accomplishment."[17] Marion was based in Paris from mid-1923 until January 1926, although every year she would spend several weeks in New York as well. Emilie Frances may have helped finance her years in France. Marion said, "For a long time Emilie Frances worked and saved—denying herself in order to help lay aside the necessary money."[18] Of course, this rather dramatic declaration is very likely an exaggeration of the actual situation, given the sisters' inheritances.

Marion studied with André Gédalge (1856–1926), who taught for years at the Paris Conservatory. A leading expert on contrapuntal technique, André Gédalge wrote a monumental book about fugue structure, which he stressed to his eager American student, although it was sometimes a frustrating topic for Marion: "…and always the eternal and sometimes infernal fugue."[19]

Marion wrote from Paris, "Like a bad penny, I always turn up sooner or later, but I know you quite understand if you do not hear from me often…. I am living a full rich life and am so deeply grateful for the opportunity of having this study and life to myself. Of course the days are not long enough to do all I want to do."[20] She studied, composed, attended concerts, wrote a few articles, and promoted her own works, distributing them to performers throughout Europe. Her compositions were also performed in Paris.[21] She became acquainted with Irving Schwerké (1893–1975), an American music critic and author who was living in Paris, who asked Marion to write her thoughts about her own music and philosophy. Speaking in the third person, Marion wrote a summary of her aesthetic goals, humbly complimented her compositional successes, and then emphasized the importance of a broad and deep knowledge. She was apparently a little uncomfortable writing praise about herself, because at the end of the document she switched to the first person and stated, "Usually my good sister Emilie Frances supplies this kind of copy for me, and I am spared the humility of 'blowing my own horn,' at any rate I have a great desire to blow an American and not a French horn."[22]

After spending a year in Paris, Marion wrote an extensive article for *The Musical Leader* about the differences between a French and an American music education, finding the latter superficial in comparison. She said, "A French child whether he shows unusual talent or not is brought up on a diet of solfege, even before taking up an instrument; by the time he is fourteen he is studying harmony seriously; by sixteen he has reached counterpoint; from eighteen to twenty-one he has covered fugue, composition, and orchestration...."[23]

Marion was largely referring to the rigorous, regimented training at the Paris Conservatory available to young music students since the Conservatory opened in 1795. The Conservatory set an entrance standard that some American students who wanted advanced studies did not meet. She may also have been reacting to feeling behind her French peers in her own education. She was, after all, about forty years old now, and had not composed an orchestral work, which for many composers is a major milestone. She had, however, composed a few larger works, such as her violin sonata and a song cycle.

About the time Marion wrote the above article, Winthrop Tryon, a music critic with the *Christian Science Monitor*, interviewed her: "This afternoon [Marion Bauer] opened out the manuscript of two of her latest piano pieces, and let me make out for myself what her year among the moderns of France has meant to her. At a glance, I could see that it signified a readjustment of harmonic method."[24] The piano pieces to which the article referred are "Quietude" (a.k.a. "Introspection") and "Turbulence." Tryon's phrase, "readjustment of harmonic methods," means that, for the first time, Marion composed bitonally (two keys simultaneously): the harmonic structure of "Quietude" is initially based on superimposed B-flat major and F-sharp minor triads. Unlike Stravinsky, whose early bitonality was often presented in loud and rhythmically driving passages, Marion's appears in a very quiet and slow movement. This piece has never been published.

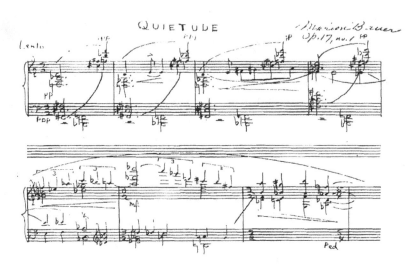

Opening measures of "Quietude."[25]

The second of the two pieces, "Turbulence," has a short, dissonant motive that pervades the entire fast-paced, edgy mood; this latter piece was finally published two decades after it was composed. Melodic dominance is a strong element in many of her previous pieces, but not in either of these new works. They are unabashedly modern. The works were performed once in Paris in 1924 (but not in America until 1942), and mentioned in *Revue Musicale*, which characterized them as showing "the magnificent progress of this composer of a moving and sensitive art."[26] Notice that Marion's first completed works after leaving New York used the harmonic grist of bitonality and atonality introduced by Schoenberg and Stravinsky (and others) with which Emilie Frances had difficulty. Perhaps the aesthetic change in Marion's music was directly linked to the physical distance between the sisters; it is easy to imagine that sharing an apartment with her esteemed sister had previously held Marion back from the experimentation that we see during her Paris years.

How Music Grew

Marion now started working on her second violin sonata (a.k.a. *Fantasia Quasi Una Sonata*, 1924–1925), and a *String Quartet* (1925–1927), both major chamber compositions that would take a year or two to complete.

But composing wasn't her only activity. During the spring and summer of 1925, Marion was in New York working with a co-author to meet a publisher's deadline on their new book.[27]

How Music Grew: From Prehistoric Times to the Present Day, begun by Marion alone, and in the end co-authored by Marion Bauer and Ethel Peyser, was issued in 1925. She and Peyser finished it at the MacDowell Colony during that summer.[28] The book's introduction, written by the music critic W. J. Henderson, described the audience they wanted to reach, "It seems to me that [the authors] have made a history of music singularly well adapted to young minds. They do not treat their readers as if they were infants––which might offend them––nor as college professors, which would certainly bore them. The book will undoubtedly have a large audience, for teachers of young music students, of whom there are legions, will surely exclaim: 'This is just what we have needed.'"[29]

Who was Ethel Rose Peyser (1882–1961)?[30] She was a native New Yorker who, during her teenage years, was sometimes mentioned in the society columns of *The New York Times*. She received her B.S. degree from Columbia University in 1908. She was a political activist who was involved in suffrage and peace marches during World War I. Peyser was on the editorial staff of the *New York Tribune* and wrote articles about maintaining a home for *Good Housekeeping, House and Garden, House Beautiful*, and other publications. She wrote a book entitled *Cheating the Junk-Pile: The Purchase and Maintenance of Household Equipment* (1922) and she had a radio program on that topic as well. During the 1920s and 1930s Peyser wrote what was essentially a gossip column for *The Musical Leader*, entitled "A-Musicking in Gotham," which was often flippant and vapid. Just how much musical knowledge she had is not clear. (Music is mentioned as her hobby in biographical sketches.) We also don't know how she and Marion became acquainted.[31] With Peyser's background and writing style, Marion's choice of her as a co-author seems odd. On the surface they appear opposites, but maybe that's the very reason they worked together: since their first book was not intended for a highly educated audience, Peyser's style might have helped create a less academic tone. Perhaps Peyser's connections with book publishers drew them together. They would later co-author two more books. Another person heavily involved in the book was Marion's sister, Flora, who was characterized as an "indefatigable and patient typist, editor and general adviser, who worked night and day for many moons."[32] *The New York Times* review of *How Music Grew* was glowing.[33]

Their book offers much in the way of valuable and congenially presented information. Today's readers, however, would be appalled by several vulgar racial stereotypes: "African" and "savage" were used interchangeably; Arabs were "barbarians"; Chinese and Japanese were "yellow races," and so forth. Isn't it ironic that a person who encountered discriminatory sexist remarks had trouble, at least initially, seeing that she was perpetrating a similar injustice? Fortunately, the later editions were revised to be more worldly and sensitive.

Fantasia Quasi Una Sonata

After Marion and Peyser completed the book, Marion remained in New York through the fall of 1925, during which time her *Violin Sonata No. 2* (a.k.a. *Fantasia Quasi Una Sonata*) premiered at a League of Composers concert. The purpose of the newly formed League of Composers was to organize and promote performances of modern music. Music critics initially received their programs with skepticism, sometimes even derision, but within a couple of years the League was a prominent and respected modern music organization. Marion's new violin sonata received a harsh review from Olin Downes in *The New York Times* (but it should be pointed out that Downes panned every other work on the program too): "[It] is seriously and sincerely composed, but the style seems to vary inconsistently between melody which is direct and diatonic and highly modern harmonies, unresolved dissonances, and the like, which sit poorly upon the principal ideas. In the form the piano has a decidedly subordinate role."[34]

Another review of the same performance was published in *The Musician*. It was more positive, and in some aspects conflicted with Downes's opinions: "It is a well constructed composition with direct utterances for both instruments."[35] Emilie Frances may have written the review of the sonata for *The Musical Leader*[36] in which the "clear clean-cut phrases and harmonic effects" and "balance between the two instruments" were praised.[37]

Winthrop P. Tryon, of the *Christian Science Monitor*, characterized the sonata as "intellectual, humorous and sentimental by turns… It argues, cajoles, appeals."[38]

The *Violin Sonata No. 2/Fantasia Quasi Una Sonata* has experimental harmonies similar to those found in her two recent piano pieces, but at the same time returns to melodic domination, though the piece is more angular in contour than those of her pre-Paris years. The melodies are direct, as Downes proclaimed, and suit the underlying harmonies well. Her harmonies vacillate between atonal and impressionist, which provide relief to each other. The primary roles of the piano are harmony, color, and rhythmic propulsion. It often accompanies the violin rather than being an equal chamber partner, creating less textural variety than we'd expect in a sonata. The best attributes of the sonata are delicious motives and poignant mood changes. The neoclassical elements of the sonata—formal structure and texture—signal the style of some her works to come.

Stravinsky

Igor Stravinsky and *Les Six* French composers (including Francis Poulenc and Germaine Tailleferre) were among the contemporary composers whose works during the 1920s–1930s are characterized as neoclassical. During Marion's first year in Paris (1923), she heard Stravinsky conduct his own works, including at the premiere of his *Octet* for wind instruments, which is neoclassical, spare, and sometimes acerbic and witty. Aaron Copland (1900–1990) was also at the concert, and reported that the audience received the work with a "general feeling of mystification," and Jean Cocteau (1889–1963; French writer and film maker who collaborated with Stravinsky) reported that the audience sat in confused silence.[39] Marion was stunned by Stravinsky's new style (as compared to the style of *The Rite of Spring*) and wrote her reaction in *The Musical Leader*: "It was slowly but surely borne in upon my mind that Stravinsky had…experimented with abstract sound utterly divorced from sentiment."[40] Marion was right. In an essay Marion wrote a year later (1924), she lucidly expanded on Stravinsky's music: "Stravinsky expresses humanism, the masses not the classes—a composer of democracy, he might be called. His pictures are impersonal;

there is no sympathy expressed with what he depicts, no attempt to preach, no opinion for or against humanity."[41] Marion's comments about Stravinsky demonstrate a keen intellect, an astute ear, and an open mind. As a composer whose own works were considered ultra-modern, she was empathetic to experimental compositions and consistently, throughout her career, she was loath to quickly condemn a style that she did not appreciate or understand. At this point in her life, she had the luxury of time to form her opinions. On the other hand, as a writer for a weekly magazine, Emilie Frances did not have the same luxury. She was also more impulsive than Marion, and she was almost one generation removed from her as well. These factors, combined with a personal writing style that was forceful and feisty, sometimes render Emilie Frances a lesser prophet than her younger sister, though never dull. An intriguing but unanswerable question is how much influence the sisters had on each other. It is easy to imagine long conversations and arguments between the two at the dinner table. It is possible that, during her younger years, Marion bowed to the opinions of her older sister, at least to a certain degree. As Marion's knowledge grew and her own tastes formed, we see her in her own light, not in Emilie Frances's shadow. That was a testament both to Marion's strength of conviction and to Emilie Frances's respect for her younger sister's judgment.

Schoenberg

Owing to Emilie Frances's long career in journalism, we are privy to the evolution of her thoughts about musical modernism. She'd certainly come a long way by 1923 and 1924, when she finally had the opportunity to hear two of the most controversial works of the early twentieth century: Schoenberg's *Pierrot Lunaire* and Stravinsky's *The Rite of Spring*.

Pierrot Lunaire was composed in 1912 and performed several times in Europe––and widely discussed in America––for nine years before its American premiere. Its atonality, "speech-song" (the singer half-speaks, half-sings), very angular melodies, unconventional instrumentation, and expressionist text were received with widespread derision. Given Emilie Frances's initial reactions to the music of Debussy and Stravinsky, it is easy to imagine that she might unleash a rant about *Pierrot Lunaire*. But by this time she had come to recognize, if nothing else, the emotional potency in modernism. After the premiere, Emilie Frances wrote, in part, "No one was lukewarm about the work; one either hated it, or was intensely moved by it. It can not be passed by with the banal remark with which most new works are greeted, that it was 'interesting.' It was expressionism with great dramatic power.... One may be stirred by the realization of originality, of a new technic of expression, and of a new plumbing of depths."[42]

Part of Emilie Frances's opinion was quoted in a 1994 article, "The New York Reception of 'Pierrot lunaire': The 1923 Premiere and Its Aftermath," in which her review was characterized as "prophetic." The author of that article stated, "Besides her oracular statement, Bauer, by evoking past and future, alludes to the chronological paradox of *Pierrot*, a work that grips the ever-shifting moment of the modern and beyond that points to the future promised by that modernity." However, the author of the article misspells Emilie as "Emile" and Frances as "Francis."[43] Was he unconsciously transforming Emilie Frances into a male critic? Shame.

The Rite of Spring

A year after the belated premiere of *Pierrot Lunaire*, Stravinsky's *The Rite of Spring* was performed (in concert, rather than as a ballet) for the first time in New York by the Boston Symphony Orchestra, conducted by Pierre Monteux. Eleven years had elapsed since its Paris premiere. Although a few in the New York audience hissed at the end of the first half, the majority responded enthusiastically.[44] Some American music critics reviewing the anticlimactic 1924 American premiere took the opportunity to summarize the history of the work and report on it in some detail. Emilie Frances commented, "[It] has the thematic beauty, tremendous sweep of orchestration, ingeniousness in creating startling effects for which Stravinsky has become the idol of the hour. It is bewildering, heavily weighted, and notwithstanding some of the dissonances without which Stravinsky will not or can not write, it has real beauty and splendor throughout."[45]

Emilie Frances had heard almost the full gamut of Stravinsky's styles to this point in his career, including his *Symphony in E-flat, L'Oiseau de Feu, Le Sacre du Printemps*, and *Three Pieces for String Quartet*, but she had not heard (as Marion had, with his *Octet*) a work in his neoclassical style. The New York premiere of Stravinsky's *Concerto for Piano and Wind Instruments* took place in 1925 (composed 1923–1924). But while the concerto (like the *Octet*) is indeed neoclassical, its spare instrumentation, very percussive piano part, and sardonic character did not appeal to Emilie Frances, "Stravinsky's piano concerto and Stravinsky's playing sounded like the music of a cave-man with a cave-man at the piano, for he went at it hammer and tongs and succeeded in getting the worst tone out of a beautiful piano that any human being ever extracted.... No one who feels good taste so offended could write intelligently of that performance, so it must just go at 'impressions.'"[46]

That Emilie Frances was in accord with other critics, such as Olin Downes of *The New York Times*, does nothing to assuage the fact that she could not appreciate any aspect of the concerto, including the lyrical slow movement. The extremely percussive piano part in the outer movements, combined with the anxiety-ridden mood, was anathema to her tastes. She alluded to the possibility that Stravinsky himself, as the piano soloist, was as much of a problem as the concerto. Given a different soloist, or some time for contemplation, would she have changed her mind about the concerto? Perhaps: a few weeks later she teased her readers with the possibility. After complaining about hearing Berlioz's *Symphonie Fantastique* twice in one week, she said she would rather hear Stravinsky's concerto again than "be compelled to hear night after night, the 'Rienzi' and the 'Tannhauser' and other overtures."[47] Was she beginning to soften her opinion about the piece? There would not be enough months left of her life for her to let us know.

All-Women Orchestra

Every time Emilie Frances went to a performance by the New York Philharmonic Orchestra, the New York Symphony Orchestra, the Philadelphia Orchestra, or the Boston Symphony Orchestra, she saw all-male participants. A woman on stage with the orchestra was a soloist like

Maud Powell or Adele aus der Ohe. The opera stages were egalitarian––they had to be––but major symphonic and operatic orchestras throughout the world were not. The purported reasons were many: women didn't play as well as men, or if they did they might become pregnant and disrupt the orchestra seating. Women would distract men. Women wouldn't look proper if they distorted their faces by blowing into a trombone or playing a violin. They were too weak to handle a rigorous rehearsal schedule. Just about every conceivable excuse was concocted for the purpose of exclusion. As a result, a few all-female orchestras formed in Europe and America. In 1924 Elizabeth Kuyper (1877–1953), a Dutch composer-violinist, formed the Manhattan-based Women's Symphony Orchestra of America, conducted by Kuyper herself. (Needless to say, women conductors were rare indeed.) When Emilie Frances first heard about the formation of the orchestra she wrote, "Analyzing what her success would mean to this country, let us draw upon our imaginations a little and visualize the thousands of young women who being good violinists and cellists have no possible outlet.... If Mme. Kuyper can succeed in interesting a body of women in placing such an organization on its feet she can be regarded as an angel of mercy who comes at a time when most needed."[48]

Kuyper's orchestra did perform a few times in New York both on stage and on the radio. Unfortunately, within a couple of years, it disbanded, owing to a lack of funds. A couple of decades later, World War II would change the landscape for women in American orchestras forever: they were hired because men were scarce, and women were finally given the opportunity to prove themselves musically.

---

[1]   Bazelon, "Woman with a Symphony," 6.

[2]   American Music Guild, concert program, 22 and 29 Apr 1922, New York, NY. Gruenberg dedicated his work for piano, "Jazzberries" (1925), to Marion.

[3]   "Works of Native Americans Heard," *MA* 36/2 (6 May 1922): 46. "Native Americans" refers to people born in America.

[4]   Marion Bauer to H. R. Austin, 8 June 1922.

[5]   "Composers Honor Mrs. Beach," *ML* 44/22 (30 Nov 1922), 483.

[6]   When I did not find it in the major libraries that house most of Marion's manuscripts, I searched in the music donated to libraries from the estates

of Albert Stoessel and Louis Gruenberg (who premiered the sonata). Albert Stoessel's son, Fredric, was also consulted. I did not find the composition, nor any leads as to whether it is still extant.

7   Marion Bauer to H. R. Austin, 21 June 1922.

8   Marion Bauer to H. R. Austin, 27 June 1922.

9   "Percy Grainger's Unusual Program," *ML* 49/3 (15 Jan 1925), 59.

10   More information about this composition is found in Appendix 1. Complete information is found at marionbauer.org.

11   Harold Morris's name is misspelled on the score as "Harald."

12   A recording of the preludes by the pianist Stephen Beus is available.

13   Richard Aldrich, "Music," *NYT*, 3 Feb 1923, 17.

14   "Marion Bauer to Sail," *ML* 45/24 (14 June 1923), 558. The author/date of the *Evening Sun* review was not provided in *The Musical Leader*.

15   A. P. S., "American Music in Paris," *ML* 47/19 (8 May 1924), 435. "A. P. S." is not Arthur P. Schmidt. The writer, then, is anonymous.

16   Marion Bauer to H. R. Austin, 27 June 1922.

17   Marion Bauer to H. R. Austin, 4 June 1923.

18   Goss, *Modern Music-Makers*, 133.

19   Marion Bauer to H. R. Austin, 27 Feb 1924.

20   Marion Bauer to H. R. Austin, 11 Nov 1923.

21   *NYT*, "Mozart in Paris," 18 May 1924, X6.

22   Marion Bauer to Irving Schwerké, 29 Jan 1925, Irving Schwerké Collection, correspondence/box, Library of Congress, Washington, DC.

23   "Superficiality the Weakness of American Musicians, Says Marion Bauer," *ML* 48/3 (17 July 1924), 56.

24   Winthrop Tryon, "American Down to the Ground," *Christian Science Monitor*, 20 Aug 1924, quoted in *ML* 48/10 (4 Sep 1924), 225.

25   More information about this composition is found in Appendix 1. Complete information is found at marionbauer.org.

26   "Revue Musicale Reviews American Works," *ML* 48/6 (7 Aug 1924), 124.

27   Emilie Frances Bauer to H. R. Austin, 3 Apr 1925.

28   "Marion Bauer Welcomed at Peterboro," *ML* 49/26 (25 June 1925), 728.

29   Marion Bauer and Ethel Peyser, *How Music Grew: From Prehistoric Times to the Present Day* (New York: G. P. Putman's Sons, 1925), xii.

30   Like Marion, Peyser lied about her age. Peyser claimed to be born in 1887, but U. S. population census records from 1890 and 1900 show she was born in 1882.

31   Their first dual authorship project was a series of essays for *Pictorial Review* in 1924–1925; like their first book, the essays were aimed at the general public.

32   Bauer and Peyser, *How Music Grew*, ix.

33   *NYT*, "Book Briefs," 17 Jan 1926, BR18.

34   Olin Downes, "Music," *NYT*, 26 Oct 1925, 19.

35   "Worth-While American Composers," *The Musician* 8 (Aug 1926), 31.

36   Whether Emilie Frances was the author of every review in the "Music in New York" section of *The Musical Leader* is not known with certainty.

37   "League of Composers Offers Unique Program," *ML* 50/18 (29 Oct 1925), 373.

38   "Marion Bauer's New Sonata," *ML* 50/14 (1 Oct 1925), 284.

39   Atlanta Symphony Orchestra, "Delta Classical Series Concert," concert program, 12 Oct 2006, Atlanta, GA.

40   Marion Bauer, "Koussevitzky and Stravinsky Conduct Paris Orchestras," *ML* 46/19 (8 Nov 1923), 430.

41   Marion Bauer, "Igor Stravinsky, A Musical Survey," *ML* 47/12 (20 Mar 1924), 277.

42   Emilie Frances Bauer, "New York Debates Merits of 'Pierrot Lunaire,'" *ML* 45/6 (8 Feb 1923), 126.

43   David Metzer, "The New York Reception of 'Pierrot lunaire': The 1923 Premiere and Its Aftermath," *MQ* 78/4 (Winter 1994): 690–692.

44   Olin Downes, "'Sacre du Printemps' Played," *NYT*, 1 Feb 1924, 12.

45   Emilie Frances Bauer, "Monteux Gives Two Concerts," *ML* 47/6 (7 Feb 1924), 134.

46   Emilie Frances Bauer, "'Ultra-Modern' Concerto Disgusts New York Audience," *ML* 49/7 (12 Feb 1925), 152.

47   Emilie Frances Bauer, "Too Much Berlioz for New Yorkers," *ML* 49/10 (5 Mar 1925), 229.

48   Emilie Frances Bauer, "Another Orchestra for New York," *ML* 47/22 (29 May 1924), 510.

CHAPTER 6

JUST TWO

Marion returned to Europe in November 1925 with the intention of staying another year. Simultaneously, the *Oregonian* published an account of Marion's career to date. It reported that "her ambition is to produce a great American opera."[1] This is the only time that ostensible fact was ever mentioned, either in interviews of Marion, reviews of her works, or her correspondence. It was much more likely she actually said her ambition was to produce a great American symphony. A decade would elapse before she would compose her first symphonic work.

Marion began with a sojourn to Italy. *The Musical Leader* reported, "She had just rounded a remarkable trip through Italy which took her to Rome, Naples, Florence, Milan, and elsewhere, in addition to Paris. She climbed Mount Vesuvius and...she spoke of being able to see nothing except steam, although she could hear the rumble of the burning lava."[2] Marion then traveled to France, where she expected to spend the next year composing and studying.

Tragedy in New York

Within a few days of Marion's arrival in Paris, Emilie Frances was hit by a car, which necessitated Marion's urgent return to America. The day after the accident, while still in Paris and making arrangements to sail to New York, Marion wrote to Austin about Emilie Frances's hospitalization, and then she commented, "For the moment, Marion Bauer the composer has been swallowed up by the writer and teacher and wage earner."[3] The tone of the letter, however, does not adumbrate that Marion feared for Emilie Frances's life.

Marion sailed on the SS *Rotterdam*, arriving in New York nearly three weeks later.[4] Emilie Frances's name continued to appear as New York correspondent for *The Musical Leader*. Whether she was able to actually attend concerts and write reviews, or whether Marion or their sister Flora took over, is uncertain: Emilie Frances's sometimes biting, sometimes effervescent style is notably absent. Marion resumed teaching piano lessons and private classes in composition, theory, and music history.[5] She had joined the newly-formed League of Composers while she was living in Paris, and on her return to America was immediately appointed to the executive board of that group.[6] Marion's acceptance of that position suggests that she realized she would be in America for some time, so perhaps Emilie Frances's condition was more precarious than Marion had initially thought. Only two weeks after her return to America, Marion learned of the death of her teacher in Paris, André Gédalge. Three weeks later, Flora's husband, R. Alexander Bernstein, died suddenly of a heart attack.[7]

Then, Emilie Frances Bauer died on 9 March 1926, a few days after her sixty-first birthday. One of her obituaries revealed her secret: "To the large public who knew Miss Bauer as a writer only, it will come as a surprise to learn the she composed under the pen name of Francesco Nogero [Francisco di Nogero]. My Love Is a Muleteer is perhaps the best-known of her songs."[8] Emilie Frances was laid to rest in the same plot as her sister, Minnie, at the Kensico Cemetery in Valhalla, New York.

Hindsight

With the benefit of hindsight, we may ask: how did Emilie Frances fare as a music critic? We are unable to judge her opinions about the quality of specific performances she heard, because recordings do not exist. On the other hand, she was almost always right in her evaluations of performers.

From pianists to singers to violinists she knew when she was hearing an outstanding performer, judging by how those performers are regarded today.

Her scorecard as a prophetess of the durability of modern music is mixed. Her sympathy for the music of Debussy, Ravel, Mahler, R. Strauss, Rachmaninov, and Puccini (to name just a few) is laudable: she quickly recognized musical immortality. Her reviews were a blend of percipient criticism and enthusiasm. Her initial condemnation of Schoenberg's music is perhaps understandable in light of being confronted with atonality for the first time, and she came to appreciate the emotional impact of his music a few years later, as we saw in her review of *Pierrot Lunaire*. Still, music criticism and prediction was her profession, so twenty-first century readers might wish she had left more of a margin for error in her initial diatribes. However, even after publishing declarative condemnations of certain modern pieces, she clearly continued to contemplate what she had heard for a long time afterward. Fortunately, she was not hesitant to state her reformed opinions later.

Regarding Stravinsky's music, some of it felt at first like a slap in the face to Emilie Frances, and she responded in kind. She certainly had plenty of company among her esteemed colleague-critics in her initial skepticism about the music of Stravinsky. On the other hand, when she heard *The Rite of Spring* for the first time, she admired it, as we have seen.

She was increasingly drawn to and sensitive toward modernism as time went on, and many of the opinions she expressed toward the end of her career hold up very well one century later. Overall, her reviews gave her readers strong opinions to contemplate, and, each week for twenty-six years, Emilie Frances crafted a balanced view of music in New York. Whether writing about grand affairs at Carnegie Hall and the Metropolitan Opera or small studio recitals and local trivia, Emilie Frances was an enthusiastic connoisseur with a significant and loyal readership.

Just Two

A month after Emilie Frances's death, Marion wrote to a friend, "I have been surrounded by tragedy and sorrow" and, mentioning that the friend had asked for a photograph of her, she said, "I have not anything yet that I can with good conscience call a likeness of myself. Some day, when I look and feel less tragic, I will tackle the problem."[9] In the same letter she mentioned that she would take over Emilie Frances's position at *The Musical Leader*, but Marion and Flora were both listed as the New York representatives, presumably sharing that position. (She used the name Flora Bauer, rather than Flora Bernstein.) Marion also revealed that she had been hired onto the New York University faculty for the following fall. It is notable that Marion secured a full-time faculty appointment so quickly, in an era when few women held such positions.

Flora

The extent of Flora's musical knowledge and experience is unknown, so exactly how much she contributed to the content of *The Musical Leader* is also a mystery. Whereas the "Music in New York" editorials sometimes used the pronoun "we" and other times used "I," the actual writing style is Marion's. Flora did belong to the Woman Pays Club, a society of professional women in the arts, and she was an associate member of the New York Chapter of the Phi Beta Fraternity for music and speech. The only prior reference to Flora's connection to music was in Minnie's obituary, which claimed Flora was "well known to the musical profession."[10] It is unknown whether she played an instrument, was a singer, or neither. She worked as a stenographer in Portland for a few years around the turn of the century, but whether she continued that occupation after she moved to New York is not known. She was married to R. Alexander Bernstein from 1914 until his death in 1926. Her nickname was "Floppy,"[11] but why? (She did enjoy wearing floppy hats, so that is one possible explanation.) One of Flora's friends, Fredric Stoessel, who was the son of one of Marion's music colleagues, described her as a "practical or business type of person"[12] and another, Jonathan Sternberg, who is a conductor and was a friend of Marion's, mentioned that Flora was about five feet one and quite rotund in her later years,[13] whereas Marion was quite tall and imposing at about five feet eight. Even though Flora was associated with *The Musical Leader* for twenty-eight years, no picture of her was found in that magazine——or anywhere else.

Shortly after the deaths of Flora's husband and Emilie Frances, Marion and Flora took an apartment together, an arrangement lasting the next twenty-eight years.[14] Jonathan Sternberg had the impression that Flora "kept house" for Marion.[15] Marion was now forty-four, and Flora was fifty-four. The two sisters were seen together so often that they were jokingly but fondly referred to by their friends as "Fauna and Flora."[16] They were the only two remaining members of the Bauer family.

Marion Bauer, College Professor

Although Marion had no formal college education, her professional accomplishments——her compositions and her book——qualified her to be hired to the position of Assistant Professor at New York University/ Washington Square College in 1926. Over the years, her courses included composition, form and analysis, aesthetics and criticism, appreciation, and history.[17] Among her early colleagues were the violinist Albert Stoessel, the musicologist Gustave Reese, and the pianist and composer Percy Grainger. Although her primary position was at New York University, she also lectured at other institutions, including Columbia University and The Juilliard School. Marion belonged to a myriad of organizations, including the League of Composers (member, Board of Directors), National Federation of Music Clubs (Chairwoman of the Young Composers Contests), and the Society of American Women Composers (co-founder with nineteen other composers, 1925).[18]

Her interests went beyond the classroom and her professional organizations: she was enamored of the power of commercial radio for promoting music in general, and modern music in particular. She was the first lecturer for the 1927–1928 New York University "College of the Air," which was a series of talks under the auspices of the Extension Division, providing free presentations to the radio-listening public.[19] She continued her radio broadcasts in New York and elsewhere[20] throughout her life. She was a commentator, a presenter of her own works (rarely personally performing at the keyboard over radio, however), and a promoter of works by other contemporary composers. She sometimes teamed with other composers, such as Aaron Copland, for on-air conversations.[21] Live performances were often part of these radio programs: "A group of compositions by Marion Bauer will be offered.... Miss Bauer will announce and direct the broadcast," read an announcement of one such program in the *New York Times*.[22]

Marion, along with artists such as Erich Leinsdorf (conductor) and Isaac Stern (violinist), took part in a weekly radio quiz show "Much Ado About Music."[23] She even participated in a blind test comparing the tone qualities of commercially sold radios. (The General Electric radio won, and afterward the headline of their advertisement was "Leaders in Music give G-E Radio overwhelming vote in tone-test," under which was a picture of the 24 judges––including Marion and George Gershwin.)[24]

Marion also lectured frequently outside of academia in New York City–– at the Chautauqua Institution in western New York, and elsewhere––on modern music and other topics, such as nationalism in music. Although she studied piano for years, she found little time to hone her performance skills, so Harrison Potter, an excellent pianist and frequent soloist in New York (as well as once at the White House), teamed with Marion in the late 1920s through the early 1940s to perform during her lectures. He championed her solo piano music on his recitals and accompanied others who performed her songs and chamber music. The close friendship among Potter, his wife, and Marion lasted until Marion's death, at which time he was the person designated to arrange for her manuscripts to be housed in various libraries and archives.

A Juggling Act

How did Marion find time to compose while she was teaching at NYU and continuing her work for *The Musical Leader*? When Syril Lee interviewed Marion for an article in the *American Hebrew*, Marion said, "I have found that I can accomplish most by working steadily and regularly. So every day I determinedly set aside three hours for this purpose [composing]––rarely ever more. Of course I must have absolute peace, but I never have to wait for inspiration." But, subsequently in the same article, Marion's own statement was contradicted: "It is only during the Summer that [Marion] now finds the leisure to do that which she loves most––compose."[25] Marion's correspondence about her compositions, and the amount of music she now produced, show that her other professional activities impinged on time previously devoted to composing.

She composed what would become one of her most celebrated works, *Sun Splendor*, at the MacDowell Colony during the summer of 1926, three months after the death of Emilie Frances. It was commissioned by the pianist Dorothy Berliner[26] who specified that it was to be the fourth piece of a rather eclectic group that included Fauré's "Clair de Lune," Griffes's "Clouds" and Debussy's "Gardens in the Rain." Marion wrote to Austin, "I personally like it very much and I feel it has a brilliant effect which of course was what I was trying to produce. It may interest you to know that I have developed––I hope spontaneously––harmonies of fifths in this piece that I have not seen anywhere else. The chord combinations instead of being groups of thirds are of fifths, six of them in a cluster. Try this on your piano––C-G-D-A-E-B. Now, have I succeeded in arousing your curiosity?"[27]

From Marion's description of the chord structure (quintal harmony, which is harmony based on stacked perfect fifths) it is clear that she was indeed one of the first composers to experiment with this sound. (One other composer who used quintal harmony as early as Marion was Ernest Bloch and then, later, Aaron Copland.) *Sun Splendor* is programmatic, based on this poem by an unknown author (possibly Marion herself):

After the storm,
Through the dispersing clouds,
Bursts forth in splendor
The Sun![28]

It is tempting to speculate that this poem depicted for Marion her feelings about emerging from her profound grief after the death of Emilie Frances.

Dorothy Berliner premiered *Sun Splendor* at Town Hall.[29] Judging from Marion's comments about the piece, as well as her pursuit of alternate versions, which she composed during the next twenty years,[30] she viewed it as one of her most important works. She must have been extremely disappointed at its premiere: the pianist was quite ill during the performance and suffered a major memory slip, bringing "the composition to an abrupt close, omitting the final climax."[31]

Sun Splendor for solo piano was never published and the music has not been located.[32] Marion was not alone in her inability to have larger works published: it was an expensive proposition. Indeed, Marion rued the difference between the publishing environment in Europe versus America: "With great regret we read that George Gershwin's Concerto in F is to be published this winter by a German publisher.... Practically all of the works by Americans in larger form either are published by European firms or remain in manuscript."[33]

She also lashed out at performing groups that were not, in her opinion, giving ample opportunities to American composers, "Isn't it discouraging when we have to face the fact that an organization which gave more than a hundred concerts this season played four American works? Isn't it disheartening to know that one organization refuses to perform [an American] work that has been presented by another organization although when the composer is a popular foreigner two organizations in a week will fight over the premiere?"[34]

The points Marion makes in the above two quotations are interconnected. Performance promotes publication and vice versa. Yet many modern works require multiple hearings to be digested and appreciated by critics and the public alike. American composers had more difficulty getting those multiple performances than their European counterparts. Marion's broad, historical views on modernism do help to put her own problems into perspective; she said, "'The new' is always at first scoffed at, looked upon as destructive and degenerate; then the chaff is separated from the wheat and the wheat is accepted, the chaff simply disappearing. Then 'the new' becomes 'the usual' and we are ready to begin the process all over again."[35]

Fantasia Quasi Una Sonata, Again

Marion's modernism played an important role in the saga of her second violin sonata, *Fantasia Quasi Una Sonata*, which was first mentioned in Chapter 5. She now gave it to Austin to show to publishers in Europe, but to no avail. (The Schmidt Company had long-standing contractual arrangements with a publishing company in Leipzig, and connections elsewhere in Europe.) She then entered it into a competition sponsored by the Society for Publication of American Chamber Music, and she complained to Austin about the puzzling result: her sonata came in first, but owing to some objections about its dissonances, a subsequent vote was taken and it then came in second. The Society usually published two works, but Marion's wasn't one of the two published that year. Marion commented, "I am not ready yet to say what I am going to do with the Sonata, when it comes home like little Bo Peep's sheep."[36]

Three months later, the situation had changed. Marion wrote to Austin, "A curious development has come up in regard to the publishing of the Violin Sonata. It seems that the committee agreed that the work 'had guts' as Mr. Tuthill said, (the words are his not mine) but some of the more conservative object to some of my dissonances. I was given to understand that if I change some of it, it would go through next year. I do not know whether to laugh or cry over such a proposition."[37] Austin immediately responded, "In a work of this kind it really seems to me that it has to stand or fall on quite other merits than the presence or absence of a few dissonances."[38]

Austin was encouraging Marion to soften some of the dissonances in her sonata so that it would be more palatable to the publisher. Marion would have to decide, then, whether those compromises would alter too radically her aesthetic goals for the piece. The foundation of this dilemma, faced by many composers, was beautifully delineated in one of Marion's lectures: "There are so many hackneyed chord combinations that composers of today would rather imply their meaning than to express it in a banal way, and...they have dropped into combinations that, to the unsuspecting and, perhaps, uninitiated listener, seem strange, forced and unsatisfying.... 'Dissonance' might be likened unto something embodying qualities of the nth dimensions, somewhat amazing in their possibilities."[39]

Finally, in 1928, G. Schirmer did publish Marion's second violin sonata, now entitled *Fantasia Quasi Una Sonata,* opus 18. Whether Marion changed the composition in order to get it published is not known for certain, but a comparison of the two extant holographs (which do have numerous crossouts and emendations) with the published version could be revealing.[40]

String Quartet

Marion had started her *String Quartet* in Paris in 1925, and she completed it in 1927. When the quartet premiered a year later, William J. Henderson wrote, "Those who like to descant upon the differences between the intellect of woman and that of man must have found themselves in difficulties while listening to Miss Bauer's quartet. It is anything but a ladylike composition. This does not mean that it is rude, impolite or vulgar, but merely that it has a masculine stride and the sort of confidence which is associated in one's mind with the adventurous youth in trousers."[41]

Marion found this account of her quartet "amusing, as well as complimentary."[42] Note, however, that even with the demise of salon music and a rise in the number of women who were serious composers (not to mention that women had won the right to vote), some music critics continued to espouse a divide between masculine and feminine music.

Ravel, Bartók, and Schoenberg

Around the same time Marion's string quartet premiered, Maurice Ravel was conducting his own compositions in New York City. Marion knew Ravel from her Paris years and attended a small post-concert gathering, which was the subject of Ethel Peyser's column, "A-Musicking in Gotham": "After the Ravel-Dale concert...we went, with Marion Bauer...to the party given for Mr. Ravel.... The feast was epicurean and there was *no* music! But instead, films of Charlie Chaplin: The Pawn Shop and One A. M. Everyone, including the delightful M. Ravel, were 'in stitches.'"[43]

Peyser reported one other humorous anecdote, "At a tea in Marion and Flora Bauer's apartment, in came Mme. Maria Kurenko with a bulldog (named Mr. Bull) as big as a small Shetland pony! The Bauers have a little Reh-Pintscher (named Tango), a little larger than a black polka dot––and at the advent of Mr. Bull (the mildest fierce looking canine we ever saw!) more doors were slammed than in a radio drama! But never the twain did meet!"[44]

Another composer who came into Marion's orbit at this time was Béla Bartók (1881–1945), who performed in New York in 1928 (and later moved there from Hungary). Although Marion did not wholly embrace his new *Piano Concerto*, at least on first hearing, she clearly admired his craftsmanship and innovation, "Bartok is, without doubt, one of the most powerful innovators of the Twentieth Century. We are now too close to him to gauge what his influence will be eventually.... Bartok is so uncompromising, so earnest in his search for primal causes...that if he penetrates only to a very small degree into our mental processes his influence will be most salutary."[45] Her reaction to his *String Quartet No. 4* was decidedly positive: "Béla Bartok's 4th Quartet...is one of the finest examples of 20th century chamber music that has come to our notice."[46] Marion correctly perceived that some of Bartók's music would survive the test of time, and also that some of it would be enigmatic to the average listener.

With Schoenberg's new twelve-tone system, Marion initially had more difficulty. The system was devilishly innovative, but Marion initially found it too mechanical, "Are we to accept this arch-geometrician, this weaver of musical patterns, this dreamer of mathematical dreams...?"[47] Looking a decade ahead for a moment, during the 1940s Marion did succumb to the lure of twelve-tone writing, which was the basis of her piano suite *Patterns*.

She clearly liked the result in that case: she arranged her piano piece for two different chamber ensembles. By the time of Schoenberg's death in 1951, Marion understood how many in the twenty-first century would perceive his niche in history. She said he was "one of the greatest innovators in the history of music," and that "it is of little importance whether his compositions live or not, because he has had such a tremendous influence on musical thinking and composing that his name will go down in history as an important source of musical development."[48] Now, more than a half-century later, we know she was right.

Ruth

During the years that Marion was on the faculty at NYU, she still spent many summers at the MacDowell Colony, where she composed and worked on her books. There, in 1929, she met Ruth Crawford (whom we mentioned in Chapter 4), who was also a gifted composer. Ruth had just experienced a secret whirlwind romance with a fellow Colonist. She turned to Marion in her emotional turmoil.[49] In her diaries, Ruth recounted her feelings about Marion: "Tho we have only just met, yet our spirits have been friends for years. We are strangers, and yet have long been friends. It is beautiful and strange.[50]

Ruth moved from Chicago to New York City in the fall of 1929, where her friendship with Marion continued. They both attended the Elizabeth Sprague Coolidge Festival in Washington, DC, where Marion "introduced Ruth to the 'influentials,' as she dubbed them." Ruth recounted: "My dear wonderful Marion Bauer...our Peterboro friendship has grown more and more beautiful. We feel like sisters. She has been a marvelous friend to me."[51]

Ruth Crawford's biographer, Judith Tick, elaborates on their relationship at that time:

> They had met at points of vulnerability for them both, each confiding the details of romantic crises. Looking back on the relationship some time later, Ruth acknowledged

how it was "like mad falling in love," and that in New York their "close constant friendship could not continue in the intensity in which it began." In Washington [DC], she believed (although Marion denied) that the two had come close to its sexual expression, retreating each in her own way from what Crawford called the "Lesbian subject." Instead, she cast their feelings into the safer molds of mother and daughter or sisters. "I am Marion's child," she wrote, perhaps missing her mother who had died eighteen months earlier. "I constantly marvel at her sisterly-motherly love for me."[52]

To further elaborate on the situation in Washington, DC, in a letter Ruth wrote to her future husband, she quoted to him what she had said to Marion:

> "Last fall in Washington," I said, "we came pretty close to it. If you had had an apartment alone in New York...I wonder?" Her answer told me that I know myself better than she knows herself....
>
> To finish quickly, ––we said goodbye in Bruxelles good friends, and I think she forgave me and understood.[53]

What was Marion's answer? That is unknown. Ruth sounds very sure of herself, but she could have been projecting her own feelings onto Marion. Thus, contradictions and innuendos swirl around few facts. As mentioned in a previous chapter, Marion wore a diamond ring on her left-hand ring finger, which is visible in two photographs of her.[54] The ring was her mother's, which was passed on to Emilie Frances, then to Marion.[55] Exactly when Marion began wearing it is unknown; she wore it to the end of her life and it fostered the false rumor of her engagement to Charles Griffes for decades after his death. It has been suggested[56] that a "bride-of-Christ" fantasy, unconscious, may be at work here, wherein Christ is not Christ (Marion is Jewish) but Griffes. Perhaps the Griffes rumor and the engagement ring permitted Marion to counter any anxiety that she might, otherwise, be viewed by the public as lesbian. Whether she was lesbian or bisexual is unknown. Indulging in speculation for a moment, two very different scenarios seem most likely. The first is that Marion was lesbian, but could not act on her desires, for fear of social stigma. The second is that Marion fell in love with Griffes, and, even though their relationship was not sexual, it fulfilled Marion profoundly––so much so that she did not seek romantic love again. The stunning absence of rumors, even among her close friends, such as Jonathan Sternberg and Fredric Stoessel, leads the author to favor the latter.

[1]   John Gratke, "Oregonians in New York," *Oregonian*, 1 Nov 1925, III3.

[2]   "Marion Bauer Returns," *ML* 51/4 (28 Jan 1926), 6.

[3]   Marion Bauer to H. R. Austin, 6 Jan 1926.

[4]   S. S. *Rotterdam* ship logs, 22 Jan 1926, www.ancestry.com (accessed 5 May 2006).

[5]   "Marion Bauer Returns," *ML* 51/4 (28 Jan 1926), 6.

[6]   "Marion Bauer Appointed to League of Composers' Board," *ML* 51/7 (18 Feb 1926), 4.

[7]   "R. Alexander Bernstein," *NYT*, 26 Feb 1926, 21. R. A. Bernstein died 24 Feb 1926.

[8]   "Emilie Frances Bauer Dies in New York," *Musical Digest* 9/22 (16 Mar 1926), 1.

[9]   Marion Bauer to Irving Schwerké, 15 Apr 1926.

[10]   "Death of Minnie Bauer," *ML* 40/10 (2 Sep 1920), 228.

[11]   Fredric Stoessel, telephone conversation with author, 18 July 2006.

[12]   Fredric Stoessel, telephone conversation with author, 18 July 2006.

[13]   Jonathan Sternberg, conversation with author, 23 June 2006.

[14]   In Melissa de Graaf's "Marion Bauer," *Contributions of Jewish Women to Music and Women to Jewish Music*, http://www.jmwc.org/Women/womenb.html (accessed 2 Aug 2006) she claims that Marion lived with her co-author, Ethel Peyser, "for some years." This is not true. Marion lived with one or several of her sisters throughout her life. Peyser lived with her mother for a few years, then with Claire Lingg.

[15]   Jonathan Sternberg, conversation with author, 23 June 2006.

[16]   Martin Bernstein, telephone conversation with the author, 11 Oct 1991.

[17]   Goss, *Modern Music-Makers*, 134.

[18]   Marion is documented to have belonged to the following organizations during her academic career: League of Composers (Board of Directors), International Society for Contemporary Music (Board of Directors, U.S. Section), MacDowell

Association (Allied Member and Corporate Member), Society for Publication of American Music (secretary, and later, Vice President), Beethoven Association, Municipal Art Committee of 100 (New York City), American Musicological Society, American Society for Comparative Musicology, National Federation of Music Clubs (Chairman of the Young Composers Contests), Society of American Women Composers (co-founder with nineteen other composers, 1925), American Music Center (co-founder, 1939), Bach Circle of New York (1930s–1940s; dedicated to performing Bach with original instrumentation), and the American Composers Alliance.

19 *NYT*, "Music Lecture Opens N. Y. U. 'Air College,'" 9 Nov 1927, 22.

20 *LAT*, "Highlights of Today's Radio Programs," 19 Jan 1932, 9.

21 Goddard Lieberson, "Over the Air," *Modern Music* XVOICE/3 (Mar–Apr 1938), 191.

22 *NYT*, "The Microphone Will Present––," 20 Sep 1931, XX11.

23 Jack Gould, "Programs in Review. 'Much Ado About Music' – Public Opinion Court," *NYT*, 7 Mar 1948, X9.

24 *LAT*, "Leaders in Music give G-E Radio overwhelming vote in tone," [advertisement], 8 Oct 1931, 7. The photograph in this advertisement is not, unfortunately, in a condition that is reproducible.

25 Syril Lee, "A Versatile Fashioner of Song. Marion Bauer Whose Compositions and Critiques are Known on Two Continents," *American Hebrew*, 6 Apr 1928, 786 and 842.

26 Her married name was Dorothy Berliner Commins.

27 Marion Bauer to H. R. Austin, 23 June 1927.

28 The poem is written out on the orchestral score, which Marion composed after the solo piano version.

29 *NYT*, "Programs of the Week," 17 Oct 1926, X6.

30 The second version is for two pianos and the third is orchestral.

31 "Young Pianist Plays Novel Program," *ML* 51/43 (28 Oct 1926), 6. Berliner did continue to perform the piece over the next twenty-five years.

32 The author contacted Dorothy Berliner Commins' children to locate her music. However, the *Sun Splendor* manuscript is not in their collection.

33 Marion Bauer and Flora Bauer, "Music in New York," *ML* 51/28 (15 July 1926), 5.

34 Marion Bauer and Flora Bauer, "Music in New York," *ML* 51/27 (8 July 1926), 5.

35 Marion Bauer, "Whither Are We Wandering With Our New Music?," *ML* 52/16 (21 Apr 1927), 10.

36 Marion Bauer to H. R. Austin, 17 Mar 1927.

37 Marion Bauer to H. R. Austin, 23 June 1927.

38 H. R. Austin to Marion Bauer, 29 June 1927.

39 "Marion Bauer in Lectures," *ML* 45/19 (10 May 1923), 448.

40 In addition to the published version, two holographs are extant. One is an incomplete draft ("opus 17") in pencil, which has only the first two movements. The other is an "opus 18" holograph, in ink, with numerous pencil emendations.

41 Goss, *Modern Music-Makers*, 132.

42 Marion Bauer to Irving Schwerké, 5 July 1928.

43 Ethel Peyser, "Meeting Ravel," *ML* 54/15 (12 Apr 1928), 14.

44 Ethel Peyser, "At Marion Bauer's," *ML* 58/16 (17 Apr 1930), 16.

45 Marion Bauer and Flora Bauer, "Bartok's New Piano Concerto," *ML* 54/8 (23 Feb 1928), 6.

46 Marion Bauer and Flora Bauer, "New Quartet by Bartok," *ML* 60/13 (26 Mar 1931), 8.

47 Marion Bauer and Flora Bauer, "Concerning the Latest Schoenberg," *ML* 57/17 (24 Oct 1929), 6.

48 Marion Bauer, "Arnold Schoenberg Passes," *ML* 83/8 (Aug 1951), 9.

49 Judith Tick, *Ruth Crawford Seeger*, 95.

50 Ruth Crawford, diaries, 1929–1930, Seeger Collection, Library of Congress, Washington, DC.

51 Judith Tick, *Ruth Crawford Seeger*, 107.

52 Judith Tick, *Ruth Crawford Seeger*, 107.

53 Ruth Crawford to Charles Seeger, [14] Feb 1931. The author has not seen the letter; its content was quoted in an e-mail message, Judith Tick to author, 13 July 2007.

54 The photographs showing the ring were taken many years after Griffes's death.

55 The diamond ring was passed on by Marion to her cousin, then to her cousin's daughter.

56 Suggested to me by a psychiatrist friend, Dr. Hilary O'Neill.

CHAPTER 7

THE GREAT DEPRESSION

Marion's NYU duties expanded some in 1930 when, with the retirement of Albert Stoessel, Marion was promoted to associate professor and appointed acting chair of the music department.[1] Under normal circumstances, a promotion in combination with taking on leadership duties would mean a salary increase. But this was during the Depression, so whether this was the case with Marion is uncertain.[2] Evidence that her own financial situation might have been affected by the Depression is contradictory: she complained about the expense of mechanical reproductions of her large works, but at the same time she was able to afford three months in Europe during the summer of 1930.

Just prior to her departure, she herself was interviewed for an article that appeared in *The Musical Leader*. While much of the interview focused on what Marion planned to see in Europe, two of Marion's comments are unusually personal for her, and are worth including here: "My sister used to say 'deliver me from living with an optimist!' but there never were two people more devoted to each other than we were,––although I see, looking back, that it must have been a strain on *her* many times." What is noteworthy here is that more than four years had elapsed since Emilie Frances's death, and yet Marion invokes her memory to explain a particular aspect of her own personality. Second, when Marion was asked whether, when she turned sixty, she might look back and have regrets, she said, "No matter what a person does, or how well he does it, there is bound to be regret for the other things he *might* have done. This is particularly so in the much-discussed instance of the woman who gives up marriage in favor of a career. I do not honestly think that there is *any* reward from professional achievement that out-weighs the other. I believe in marriage."[3] Marion could have answered the question regarding professional accomplishments in a myriad of ways. But she didn't. Her regret was highly personal. In all of the information about Marion, including that information she herself provided, this is the only instance where she revealed that, in giving up a personal relationship in favor of a career, she felt a sense of loss. The interviewers were seemingly both uncomfortable and surprised by Marion's response, evidenced by their hasty change to a different topic. Nina Naguid, of *The Musical Leader*, published another article about Marion that offers further perspective on her personality. Naguid described a "discernible twinkle in her eye, placed there by an unusual capacity for fun, [and] an inimitable wit." She also characterized Marion as having "a dazzling intelligence."[4]

Europe, 1930

Marion began her European sojourn in England, where she heard the New York Philharmonic, under the direction of Arturo Toscanini, perform in Albert Hall, which she described as "one of the most impressive concerts within my experience."[5] (The orchestra was just completing an extensive tour of Europe.) She celebrated the Fourth of July at Fontainebleau, France, where the American Conservatory had been established by Walter Damrosch ten years earlier, and where Nadia Boulanger taught for decades.[6] (Boulanger was discussed in Chapter 2.) Just as Marion arrived in Bayreuth, Germany, Siegfried Wagner died. (Siegfried was Richard Wagner's son, and for two decades he had been in charge of the Wagner festival there.) Marion found the city in mourning. She paid her respects at the Wagner home, Villa Wahnfried, and at Richard Wagner's grave:

> Seeing for the first time the beautiful villa, the grave, the utter peace and beauty of the castle gardens…made me feel that Bayreuth was the kind of an apotheosis for Wagner such as few humans have ever been privileged to experience. Of course he was a genius, and of course he

had suffered as few are made to suffer in this none too easy world…."[7]

Marion was surely cognizant of Wagner's anti-Semitism; she, then, like some other Jewish musicians, must have been willing to bear that burden for the sake of his Art.

From Bayreuth, she went to Oberammergau, Austria, to see the famous Passion Play, which she found to be a thrilling artistic production.[8] She visited Nürnberg, Germany, to see the "home of *Die Meistersinger*," and while there she ran an old friend, Serge Koussevitzky (1874–1951), who was conductor of the Boston Symphony Orchestra.[9] Marion's final stop in Europe was Liège, Belgium, where she attended the festival of the International Society for Contemporary Music. There the highlight for Marion was hearing Berg's opera, *Wozzeck*, for the first time. (The opera had premiered five years earlier in Europe, but had not yet been performed in America.) Marion commented that Berg had "created an atmosphere which is at once novel and satisfactory. The effect is so gripping that the auditors, even those who are not admirers of atonality, forget that they are listening to an atonal opera. Perhaps nothing could attest to Berg's achievement more conclusively than this."[10] At the other end of the spectrum, she heard works she did not admire: in one of her rare moments of not tempering her critical language, she said that Alexander Mossolow's work, entitled *Steel Foundry*, "was about as pleasant an experience as being in a boiler factory."[11]

On a personal note, Marion connected again with Ruth Crawford in Liège. Ruth confided to Marion that she was now involved with Charles Seeger (who was married to someone else at the time). Ruth was in the mood for solitude, but Marion needed to talk to a friend. Unfortunately, we don't know what was on Marion's mind, but Ruth's description makes it sound personal: "There were things she hadn't been able to talk to anyone about for months, and she needed to talk. Even as I needed silence."[12] Was Marion confessing her own romantic encounter since she last saw Ruth? Was this what was really on Marion's mind when she commented about marriage in the interview? Only Ruth knew, and she didn't tell us.

After spending just over three months in Europe, Marion boarded a ship in Cherbourg, France, for the twenty-one day trip back to New York to resume teaching and composing.[13]

Shortly after Marion returned from Europe, she and Ethel Peyser began a new book, *Music Through the Ages: A Narrative for Student and Layman*, which was published in 1932. The authors described its purpose in their introduction: "Music Through the Ages is designed as a tool for the student to pick out the salient points in the long and vivid story of music, with no intention to be encyclopedic. Although primarily for the student, it is written also with the idea of enticing the layman and stimulating him to acquire authentic information about the varying phases of music since its genesis through the era in which he lives, and to leave with him some inkling as to what may come in the future."[14] The book received excellent reviews, but whether Marion benefited to any great degree from royalties is not known. The next year, 1933, Marion published yet another book, but she was the sole author: *Twentieth Century Music: How It Developed, How to Listen to It*. It received several rave reviews, including one from William J. Henderson, who said, "The book is the first important American contribution to the study of the new music. It is valuable for that reason. It is even more valuable because the author has written with full understanding, with authority, with sympathy and with the benefit of long experience as a lecturer and teacher."[15] Marion also published a companion pamphlet to that book, *A Summary of Twentieth Century Music* (1935), which was designed to facilitate its use in the classroom.

During some of the darkest days of the Great Depression, a couple of events probably brought cheer to Marion, although she didn't comment on them much in her correspondence. First, the Metropolitan Opera star, Leonora Corona, performed Marion's song "Orientale" on a gala concert. Marion orchestrated the song for the concert and Corona was accompanied by the Metropolitan Opera Orchestra.[16] Second, Whitman College bestowed upon Marion an honorary masters degree in June 1932. She almost declined the invitation to accept the degree because of the expense of a continental train trip. In the end, though, she accepted, and enjoyed her only known visit back to her hometown of Walla Walla.[17] She also visited Portland, Oregon, during the same trip, where she lectured on "Music in the Twentieth Century." During an interview for the *Oregonian*, she mentioned that another composer, Gena Branscombe, also received an honorary masters from Whitman College at the same ceremony. (Branscombe briefly taught at Whitman College at the turn of the century.) She went on to say, "Miss Branscombe, Mrs. H. H. A. Beach, and I are known as the triad of American women composers, and are sometimes referred to as the 'three B's of music.'"[18] (Marion is joking here, of course, because the usual "three B's" are Bach, Beethoven, and Brahms.) Marion designated Amy Beach as "the outstanding woman composer of America" and Gena Branscombe "a close second."[19]

During the Depression, Marion visited the MacDowell Colony less frequently, or interrupted her Colony work to lecture elsewhere. She taught summer sessions at various institutions, each session lasting between two and six weeks: Mills College (1935; Oakland, CA), the Carnegie Institute (1936 and 1939; Pittsburgh, PA), Cincinnati Conservatory (1938), Teachers College of Columbia University (1940), and The Juilliard School (1941; 1944-1955). Marion loved teaching, so the summer sessions were probably welcomed––and remunerative––but above all she wanted to compose and no doubt missed the repose of spending an entire summer at the Colony. In addition, The Chautauqua Institute[20] became part of her summer schedule. Some summers she was music critic for the *Chautauquan Daily*. Most of Marion's lectures in New York City were about contemporary music, but at Chautauqua they were more varied, such as "Innovators of the Nineteenth and Twentieth Centuries: Beethoven as Romanticist"; "How Schumann Related Music to the Other Arts"; "A Comparison Between Chopin and Debussy"; "The Influence of Bach on Cesar Franck"; and "Music in the Americas."[21]

Sun Splendor, Again

Marion revisited her composition *Sun Splendor* during the early 1930s. Undaunted by publishers' refusals of the original solo piano piece, she composed a two-piano version which premiered at Town Hall in 1931, with Germaine Schnitzer and Ignace Hilsberg, pianos.[22] It was performed again in 1933 by Claire Ross and Alice Griselle,[23] and in 1934, again at Town Hall by the famed duo-pianists Guy Maier and Lee Pattison.[24] On at least seven occasions over the next four years Marion tried to persuade Austin to publish it, but without success.[25] In her final plea to him she sounded dejected, "I know there is not much money in two-piano music but after Maier and Pattison played my 'Sun Splendor,' I should love to have it published. Is there any chance that you could do it? I have had a few requests for it, and, of course, I cannot keep on sending people photostats because they are too expensive. It has been a long time since I have seen my name on the front of any new composition and it is a bit discouraging."[26]

The two-piano version was also never published, but a holograph is extant. Given that the solo piano score is missing, the two-piano version is the closest representation of the original we have. Over the next decade, Marion orchestrated *Sun Splendor*, and, in its final version, the piece would represent the height of her career.

Overall, her compositional output during the early 1930s was relatively low in sheer numbers because, compared to her shorter songs, several of the works were lengthy and more complex: *Dance Sonata* for solo piano, *Sonata for Viola or Clarinet and Piano*, *Duo for Oboe and Clarinet*, and *Four Songs with String Quartet*.

Her extended thoughts about song-writing at this point in her career are found in her letters to the American musician and author William Treat Upton (1870–1961). In 1931, she wrote:

> I became discouraged about writing songs because I found so little response or musicianly understanding on the part of the singers, and their unwillingness to work out the songs of American composers. But this does not mean that I have not written songs and do not intend to write more.[27]

In 1932, she added:

> Another difficulty in modern song writing has been poetic texts. With few exceptions, the poets of today are seeking

new idioms, just as musicians are, and their poetry does not lend itself to the old musical forms. But here lies a fascinating problem and one which will probably lead to a new type of song-writing in keeping with the modern chamber music and orchestral works.[28]

The songs that Marion wrote during the summer of 1932 were much more modern than had been her previous style. One example, "To Losers," was composed at the MacDowell Colony. The song is dated "Aug. 15th, 1932," her fiftieth birthday. Was she telling us how she felt about turning fifty? Frances Frost wrote the text of "To Losers": "And if you lose be still / As a stricken hawk upon a granite hill, / The great wings broken. / Be mute, / The rock will yield a hollow / Uncomforted by fern for the hours that are to follow / Accuse the heart for what you lose / The heart–that wild dark bird of haste thinking it heard / What was not spoken, / Leaving the climbing emptiness of air / And falling to the voice that was not calling / To the breast that was not there."[29]

The initial four-note motive, D#-E-B-C, is the basis for both the melody and harmony throughout the song. The motive's two minor seconds (D#-E and B-C), create dissonant harmonies. The vocal line, in the alto range, is more angular and more difficult to perform than those in her previous songs. The mood of "To Losers" is pervasively somber and dark. Joan Peebles (1899–1991), a singer with the American Opera Company, premiered it. A review stated, "There is much meat in [the song] and it says a lot in a few measures. Words and music have rarely been matched to better advantage, for the style of both poem and music is identical."[30] William Treat Upton singled out the song for its "technical skill and harmonic freedom."[31] The song was not published during Marion's lifetime.

Last measures of "To Losers" with the place and date of composition at the end.

Another song of Marion's from the same time is "When the Shy Star Goes Forth." Its mood is lighter, and it is less dissonant, but the melodic line is similarly angular. Here Marion can be commended for the quality of the text––by James Joyce (from *Chamber Music*).

In Marion's *Fantasia Quasi Una Sonata* (1924–1925) for violin and piano, she had begun to head toward a neoclassical style. During the 1930s, she fully embraced it in her chamber music. Like many other composers, she looked back to the classical period for formal structures (such as the sonata) and for a sparer texture. Classical chamber instrumentations enjoyed more attention with the advent of the neoclassical style (as opposed to the large orchestral works so prevalent in the first quarter of the twentieth century). Baroque counterpoint––the weaving together of two or more lines of equal importance––was resurgent, with modern harmonies. Her *Duo for Oboe and Clarinet* (1932) exemplifies neoclassicism and was her first exploration of writing for wind instruments. Most composers do not write in a vacuum––Marion likely came to know wind players who were interested in performing her works. In this case, faculty and students at NYU were the first performers. The choice of the rare duet combination of oboe and clarinet allows the two instruments to simultaneously play in the

159

same register and still be aurally independent because of their very different timbres. The first movement, "Prelude," is jovial, beautifully exploring combinations of the two instruments. It is a canon at the fourth (with a two-measure delay) which midway through is inverted. In contrast, the slow-paced second movement, "Improvisation," begins with a melancholy solo clarinet statement that is answered in kind by the oboe. While the first movement is more rhythmically active and predictable, the second movement sounds, as the title states, like an improvisation. The third movement, "Pastoral," is related to the first movement in its moods and rhythms, but with appealing new melodies. The last movement, "Dance," features quick interactions between the two instruments––like two people dancing together. This duo deserves to be in today's repertoire.

PRELUDE

Opening of "Prelude" from *Duo for Oboe and Clarinet* (canon at the fourth).[32]

Prometheus Bound (1929) also features an unusual instrumentation: two flutes and two pianos. It was conceived as incidental music for Aeschylus's play of the same name for a live performance with the Greek Stage Society of New York University.[33] However, it appears from an article in *The Musical Leader* that Marion thought the music could also stand independently of the play: "Miss Bauer's music…is expected to arouse considerable comment, not so much because of the fact that, though interpreting a Greek tragedy she keeps to her use of the modern idiom as that the music in itself is felt to be a significant contribution to modern American music."[34] Unfortunately, the score of *Prometheus Bound* has not been found. Marion's continuing intrigue with flute, and with Greek modes, is evident in her 1936 work *Five Greek Lyrics* for solo flute. Each of the five captivating vignettes features a different mode. These were written for and premiered by Georges Barrère (1876–1944), who was principal flautist of the New York Symphony Orchestra for decades, and whose influence on American flute playing was immense. The only holograph that has been found appears to be a rough draft. For the historian, whether a holograph is a complete and final draft is not always clear. If it's in ink, neatly written, with few or no revisions, it seems more finished. In this case, the holograph is obviously a rough draft because the titles of the movements are different than the titles that were published in the program at the time of its premiere. There are numerous revisions in the holograph, with Marion's notes to herself in the margins. Still, the holograph is viable, and the piece could, and should, be reconstructed. Of course Georges Barrère received a finished holograph for his performance, but it is not part of his archive.[35] Other works involving wind instruments include her *Sonatina* for oboe and piano (1938–1939), *Concertino* for oboe, clarinet, and string quartet (1939–1943; this is an expansion of the *Sonatina*), and her *Sonata* for clarinet or viola and piano (1932 or 1935).

Marion was able to get several of her latest works performed during the Depression and, in general, she was much more fortunate than many musicians during that time. In 1934, she commented at length about the suffering of the public, musicians, and the arts. She pointed out that most American composers were now not able to make a living by writing music. Furthermore, children who would have been given music lessons in easier economic times were deprived of this luxury, which also meant that those who earned a living by offering private music lessons were under duress. Marion was especially concerned about children not being able to play in school ensembles or sing in choruses, and the ramifications therein on the future of music in America.[36]

She was optimistic about that fact that radio was the free entertainer, as it were, during the Depression. For composers like Marion, who were fortunate enough to have their works broadcast, it was also an important professional tool. Marion frequently participated in live radio programs in

New York. She was also a commentator at the Library of Congress Festival of Chamber Music in 1933. During that broadcast, wrote Nina Naguid, "She was told to ad lib for eight minutes, which she did with but a second's hesitation."[37]

During the Depression, live public performances were often too expensive for an individual or a group to organize. That problem was addressed by the Works Projects Administration's (WPA) Federal Music Project. The WPA had a Music Education Division, which, in 1935, instituted a "composers' forum-laboratory" in order "to provide an opportunity for serious composers, residing in America, both known and unknown, to hear their own compositions, to test the reactions of auditors, as well as to present their own particular viewpoint...and benefit by a public discussion of their works."[38] Each forum audience member was given a slip of paper on which to write questions or comments about the program, which provided the basis for a post-concert discussion with the composer, assisted by a moderator.

Marion, Aaron Copland, Roy Harris, Morton Gould, and many other composers jumped at the chance to participate. Marion was the first woman chosen to do a presentation, which she entitled "The Evolution of a Composer." For the program she chose works that demonstrated changes in her compositional style over two decades. In 1936, she was invited back to give a second presentation, which included her most important chamber works to date and a song cycle: *Fantasia Quasi Una Sonata* (1924–1925); *Four Poems*, opus 16 (1922) for voice and piano; *Sonata for Viola (or Clarinet) and Piano* (1932 or 1935; this may have been its New York premiere); and *String Quartet* (1925–1927).

Fortunately, each question-answer session between the composer and audience was transcribed. The transcript[39] from the 1936 concert reveals that Marion reacted mildly negatively to audience questions about the structure of her music. For example, when asked about the structure of her second violin sonata, she referred the person who posed the question to the program notes, and then she commented, "I knew what I was doing. I did not strike out wildly. I planned it carefully and when it came to analyzing it to myself, I could do it to my own satisfaction."

When asked whether she approved of nationalism in music, she laughed, and then said, "I do not believe in it slavishly. I do not believe that we can say it is not 'American' because it does not reflect the Negro, Indian, Cowboy or our Plains. What do people expect? What do they want? What is 'American'?... To seek nationalism is, perhaps, not as artistic as some people believe."

One audience member asked Marion to "account for the relative scarcity of women composers," to which she responded, "There are a great many more than you think," and then she laughed and said, "Just think of us as composers and never call us lady composers."

At the end of the question-answer session, written compliments from the audience members were read aloud. The last one said, "My warm congratulations may be best expressed by telling you that your program tonight fulfills the high hopes and belief of your sister––Emilie Frances."

---

1   Anabel Parker McCann, "Woman Heads Music Department of New York University," *New York Sun*, 24 Nov 1930, quoted in *ML* 59/23 (4 Dec 1930), 5.

2   Salaries, even long ago, are considered private information by the NYU administration.

3   Emelyn Paige, "An Interviewer Interviewed," *ML* 58/22 (29 May 1930), 16.

4   Nina Naguid, "The Versatile Marion Bauer," *ML* 60/24 (11 June 1931), 61.

5   Marion Bauer, "Triumphant Tour Closes. Marion Bauer Writes of Toscanini and His Men––Ponselle Remarkable as Ever––Coincident in London," *ML* 58/25 (19 June 1930), 3.

6   Marion Bauer, "Fourth of July Celebrated at Fontainebleau," *ML* 59/4 (24 July 1930), 3. Nadia Boulanger became director of the school in 1948.

7   Marion Bauer, "At Bayreuth," *ML* 59/8 (21 Aug 1930), 3.

8   Marion Bauer, "Impressions of Oberammergau," *ML* 59/11 (11 Sep 1930), 3.

9   Marion Bauer, "We Meet Koussevitzky," *ML* 59/11 (11 Sep 11 1930), 4.

10 Marion Bauer, "Alban Berg's 'Wozzeck,'" *ML* 59/14 (2 Oct 1930), 10.

11 Marion Bauer, "Second Symphonic Concert," *ML* 59/14 (2 Oct 1930), 10.

12 Ruth Crawford to Charles Seeger, [14] Feb 1931. The author has not seen the letter; its content was quoted in an email, Judith Tick to author, 13 July 2007.

13 SS *America* ship log, 10 Sept 1930, www.ancestry.com (accessed 30 May 2007).

14 Marion Bauer and Ethel Peyser, *Music Through the Age: A Narrative for Student and Layman* (New York: G. P. Putnam's Sons, 1932), xi.

15 "Critics Hail Marion Bauer's New Book," *ML* 66/26 (19 May 1934), 11.

16 *NYT*, "Sing 'Old Favorites' at Opera Concert," 28 Mar 1932, 10.

17 Marion Bauer to Stephen Penrose, President of Whitman College, 18 Feb 1932. Penrose Library, Archives, Whitman College, Walla Walla, WA.

18 *Oregonian*, "America Moving Up in Music Field, Noted Composer Says," 6 June 1932, 2.

19 Anabel Parker McCann, "Woman Heads Music Department of New York University," *ML* 59/23 (4 Dec 1930), 5. The *ML* article quoted from an article in the *New York Sun*, 24 Nov 1930.

20 The Chautauqua Institute, in southwest New York state, is a summer institute for fine arts, performing arts, and literary arts and includes performances, lectures, and classes. The presentations draw tens of thousands of visitors through the summer.

21 "Stoessel Directs Music at Chautauqua," *ML* 69/13 (Aug 1937), 2 and 4.

22 W. B. C., "Two Pianists Play Novelties," *NYT*, 9 Mar 1931, 25.

23 Nina Naguid, "Emily Roosevelt and Duo-Pianists," *ML* 65/21 (23 Nov 1933), 2. Author is "N. N."

24 *NYT*, "Programs of the Week," 18 Nov 1934, X6.

25 Marion Bauer to H. R. Austin, 17 Dec 1930; 1 July 1931; 10 Aug 1931; 28 Nov 1931; 12 Apr 1932; 14 Dec 1932; undated [late 1932 or early 1933].

26 Marion Bauer to H. R. Austin, undated [late 1932 or early 1933].

27 Marion Bauer to William Treat Upton, 18 Nov 1931, William Treat Upton Collection, correspondence/box, Library of Congress, Washington, DC.

28 Marion Bauer to William Treat Upton, 3 May 1932.

29 Text taken from music score. More information about this composition is found in Appendix 1. Complete information is found at marionbauer.org.

30 "Chautauqua Season Closes," *ML* 65/9 (31 Aug 1933), 3.

31 William Treat Upton, "Aspects of the Modern Art Song," *MQ* 24/1 (Jan 1938): 29.

32 More information about this composition is found in Appendix 1. Complete information is found at marionbauer.org.

33 "Aeschylus in English," *NYT*, 29 Dec 1929, 23.

34 "Prometheus Bound," *ML* 57/23 (5 Dec 1929), 15.

35 His archive is at the New York Public Library for the Performing Arts.

36 David Hazen, "Noted Authority on Music, Ex-Portland Girl, Visitor," *Oregonian*, 2 June 1934, 12.

[37] Nina Naguid, "Marion Bauer in New Role," *ML* 64/18 (4 May 1933), 8.

[38] *NYT*, "Composers' Forum-Laboratory," 29 Sep 1935, X7.

[39] Composers' Forum-Laboratory, Transcript of the Tenth Program, Marion Bauer, Composer, Ashley Pettis, Director, 8 Jan 1936. The transcript is at the New York Public Library for the Performing Arts, New York, NY. All quotations are drawn from this transcript.

CHAPTER 8

FINALE

The American Music Center was founded in 1939 by Marion Bauer, Aaron Copland, Howard Hanson, Quincy Porter, Otto Luening, and Harrison Kerr. They founded it in response to American composers having difficulty getting their works published and distributed, and performers having problems finding the music. As a central communications center for American music it proved to be invaluable to the cause. Today, it is still a thriving organization, maintaining a library of more than 55,000 scores and recordings representing the work of over 8,000 composers.[1] After Marion's own music, the Center is among her most prominent legacies.

Marion was also a long-standing member of the League of Composers. An incident at a concert put on by the League highlights Marion's ingenuity. A blizzard prevented the scheduled performers from arriving in New York City in time. Yet, a capacity audience had braved the weather. The organizers of the concert began to panic. Just minutes before the concert was to begin, Marion noticed the famed pianist, John Kirkpatrick, in the audience and, explaining the situation to him, asked him if he would play the Charles Ives sonata which Marion had heard him perform a week earlier. He happily agreed to do so. Immediately thereafter she encountered a chamber group that was to premiere Aaron Copland's *Sextet* later that day; they had their instruments with them, so Marion asked them if they would be willing to have an "extra rehearsal" in front of the audience, and they, too, readily agreed. The concert was reported to be spectacular.[2]

Stunning News

Taking into account Emilie Frances's career with *The Musical Leader*, the magazine had been part of Marion's and Flora's lives in one way or another for almost four decades, which rendered this August 1939 announcement especially shocking: in a published letter to the owner of the magazine, Florence French, Marion and Flora "with deep regret" resigned their positions. They characterized their many years with the magazine as "happy and profitable," and wished Florence French "great success and prosperity."[3]

On the same page that their letter appeared, *The Musical Leader* published "A Message of Appreciation," probably penned by Florence French, that included this: "Year after year they have carried on the work begun by their famous sister Emilie Frances Bauer who, when this paper was founded, became its Eastern representative.... After Emilie Frances died, her sisters Marion and Flora undertook to carry on the work and this they have done with the utmost efficiency."[4]

Then, six months later, without any explanation, Flora alone returned as New York Representative,[5] a position she retained until 1954. Marion contributed essays, including in a regular column entitled "According to Marion Bauer," and she wrote occasional reviews. What happened? The extreme brevity of the Bauer sisters' letter bespeaks anger. About what? Money? Does the use of both "profitable" and "prosperity" in one short letter mean something? Are there hidden messages in *The Musical Leader's* response? Why was Emilie Frances called "famous" whereas Marion and Flora were "efficient"? Why wasn't Flora's return a few months later at least announced in a brief paragraph? No business records or correspondence for *The Musical Leader* were found to answer these questions. What is clear is that Marion's compositional output accelerated during the next few years, and she published a new book and revised a previously published book.[6]

New Books and Compositions

Her new book, *Musical Questions and Quizzes*, was published in 1941.[7] The book presents a lighthearted approach to music trivia. There are questions about opera characters, singers, composers, and so forth. For example, "Which composer wrote a song on his shirt sleeve?" (The answer is Franz Schubert.) Marion dedicated the book "to my sister Flora Bauer who has been a patient victim of these Questions and Quizzes." Within the next few years, Marion completely revised and brought up-to-date her previously published book, *Twentieth Century Music*.

The 1940s brought some of Marion's largest compositions, including several orchestral works: *Symphonic Suite for String Orchestra* (1940), *Piano Concerto* (1942), *Sun Splendor*, which is a symphonic poem for orchestra (1934–1946), *Prelude and Fugue* for flute and string orchestra (1948), and *Symphony No. 1* (1947–1950). After going through several years of atonal and bitonal writing, Marion returned to a loosely tonal idiom in her first major orchestral work, *Symphonic Suite for String Orchestra*. In three movements, the piece has some glorious passages, but it could be criticized for its texture: all the instruments play with little rest and in a limited register throughout each movement. Some enticing melodies are lost within the thick and complex setting. Those problems disappear in her next orchestral work, *Piano Concerto* ("American Youth"). She composed it in 1942 with a high school or college soloist in mind, so it is of moderate technical difficulty and is of modest length for a three-movement work, at about sixteen minutes. It received a complimentary review after its premiere in 1943, "Miss Bauer's concerto again proves that the great past need not be neglected when writing in the modern idiom.... Romanticism...permeated the entire composition."[8]

The concerto may have been the first piece Marion composed for full orchestra.[9] Its pervasive lyricism and diatonicism are a surprise, given Marion's style over the preceding decade. The first movement is lyrical and romantic. The romanticism comes from the large orchestra combined with tonal and diatonic writing. Modernism is manifest rhythmically and, occasionally, harmonically. The piano and orchestra explore wide pitch ranges, a variety of melodies and rhythms, and changing moods. Her handling of the interplay between the piano and orchestra is adroit. The second movement was a development of an earlier piano piece, but it is unknown which one. Here, the harmonies are somewhat more impressionistic, but the orchestration and rhythmic structures unify this movement with the first. Its moods range from placid to soaring. If there were any doubt in the listener's mind about the Americanism of this concerto in the first two movements, none would remain after hearing the last movement's boogie-woogie rhythm. While the opening of the last movement is less sophisticated artistically, the interplay between the piano and orchestra is skillful. The middle section features a saxophone announcing a spiritual-like melody, providing a welcome contrast to the opening in color, mood, and tempo. The movement then returns to the boogie-woogie theme. Is this a masterpiece? No. Is it worth having in today's repertoire for younger pianists? Yes.[10]

Marion composed her *Piano Concerto* during World War II. Whether she had any relatives still remaining in her parents' native Alsace is unknown; if she did, they would have been obvious Nazi targets. It's probably not a coincidence that Marion composed her only known religious work, "Benediction," for voice and organ, during World War II.[11] A review noted that its "expressive melody was filled with the spirit of profound religious devotion."[12] It was performed by the cantor at Temple Emanu-El in New York City. (Jewish services use the term "benediction," particularly for the "priestly" blessing, with the text from Numbers 6:23-27,[13] which is the text of Marion's song.) It has a foreboding sound, most especially in the middle of the song, with repeated tritones in the bass register. Only at the final "amen" does the mood lift with the resolution of the insistent dissonance into a major triad.

Middle of "Benediction" with bass register tritones.[14]

In 1942, when Marion was asked what she thought a composer's wartime function was she responded, "To try to compose works that would be timely, principally choral numbers, that might be used in…concerts throughout the country; to carry on as far as possible, a normal composing program in order to have works for the future and to keep up the interest, which has obviously increased, in American composition."[15]

Her contribution to the choral literature at this time was *China*, with a text by Boris Todrin. It premiered at the Worcester Festival in 1945, performed by the Worcester Festival Chorus and Philadelphia Orchestra. In a review in *The Musical Leader* we learn that Marion was thrilled with the performance: 350 singers in the chorus and an "impeccable" performance by the Philadelphia orchestra.[16] Marion's holograph for chorus and piano has been located, but her expanded version for chorus and orchestra has not.[17]

In 1946, Marion composed using the twelve-tone (serial) system for the first time in her career, in her solo piano piece, *Patterns*. Arnold Schoenberg brought out the compositional technique in 1923, but some composers (such as Stravinsky, Copland, and Marion) did not employ it until later. Marion was suspicious of serial writing when it first emerged, intimating that the mathematical nature of the system was antithetical to making music; she obviously later changed her mind. *Patterns* for solo piano has five brief movements, totaling about twelve minutes. When it premiered in 1947,[18] a review in the *New York Herald Tribune* reported, "Miss Bauer's 'Patterns' were deftly wrought and employed the twelve-tone scale without the acridity which is sometimes associated with it."[19] Why Marion decided to suddenly experiment with serial writing is unknown, but she liked the result, judging from her subsequent arrangements of the piece for a chamber ensemble (two each of flutes, oboes, clarinets, bassoons, horns, plus string bass); she also arranged all five movements for string quartet (in this case, the title is *Five Pieces for String Quartet*, 1946–1949). Her piano work *Moods* (1950) is also twelve-tone.

Opening of the first movement of *Patterns*. The movement is notable for its clear-cut tone-row and contrapuntal texture.[20]

One of Marion's best songs from this time is "Swan," on a text by Edna Castleman Bailey about a dying swan. Marion returned to the repetitive accompaniment pattern that was characteristic of her earlier songs, but here with neoimpressionist harmonies. Although the text is not exactly religious, it ends with, "There is still God, there is still my own soul," which

Marion depicted exquisitely. A brief piano coda sounds like a puff of smoke disappearing into air. Another song from the same time, "The Harp," was aptly characterized by Charles Mills as "a splendid lyric achievement, probably one of the best contemporary American pieces in the medium."[21] The premiere took place in 1943, sung by the famed baritone Yves Tinayre, with Harrison Potter on piano, over WQXR radio in New York City.[22]

Sun Splendor, Orchestrated

A surprising feature of these pieces from the 1940s is Marion's use of very divergent harmonic styles, from tonal to neoimpressionist to twelve-tone. At the same time, Marion revised an older work: *Sun Splendor.* It had been conceived in 1926 as a solo piano work; her two-piano version followed in 1930; working sporadically from 1934–1947, she orchestrated it. In its final form, *Sun Splendor* is a symphonic poem for orchestra. On 25 October 1947, the New York Philharmonic, conducted by Leopold Stokowski, performed it in Carnegie Hall.

Francis Perkins wrote in the *Herald Tribune*, "The orchestra is skillfully utilized, and instrumental and harmonic color and evocation and contrast of mood more than the musical ideas themselves, are the salient points of the composition."[23] The critic for *The New York Times* was lukewarm: "It is a five-minute sketch depicting the rising of the sun…. Miss Bauer was certainly not unfamiliar with Ravel's sunrise music from 'Daphnis and Chloe' when she wrote it, but she has added a few descriptive orchestral touches of her own. The piece was vivid enough, but the sun seemed barely up before the number was over."[24]

None of Marion's versions of *Sun Splendor* were published and no commercial recordings are available. A recording of the New York Philharmonic performance is in their archive, which, owing to union rules, can be heard only in that venue.[25] The holograph was housed in the Mt. Holyoke College archives, but has apparently been lost.[26]

Retirement

Marion retired from New York University in the spring of 1951. That same year, Marion and Flora were surprised not to receive a royalty check for Emilie Frances's song! Marion wrote, "For the first time in a good many years we received no Christmas present of a royalty from 'My Love is a Muleteer.' Has this too gone to sleep?"[27] Marion would be sixty-nine years old that August. The mandatory retirement age was sixty-five, so perhaps she claimed to NYU that her birth-year was 1886.

She continued in her post as National Music Adviser to the Phi Beta Fraternity, a professional co-educational fraternity for people in the performing and creative arts. Over the years Marion had also contributed many articles to the Phi Beta magazine, *The Baton*. The March 1951 issue was "respectfully dedicated to Marion Bauer"[28] and was devoted to her career. It included a lengthy interview of Marion by Irwin Bazelon:

> Miss Bauer, who has recently completed a seventeen minute Symphony, is one of the very few women composers to have written a large work in symphonic form, or for that matter, to be actively engaged in music composition as a serious creative endeavor in direct competition with her male compatriot composers. Specializing in chamber and pianoforte music, she has contributed many scores to the musical literature of American music, a literature not overly abundant with works by women composers. The latter group is not as rare a phenomenon as one would believe, but those that are taken seriously by the male fellow-artists are indeed a select and designated minority. Her completely musical life, augmented by teaching, writing and lecturing, in addition to her composing activities, is a distinct rebuttal to those die-hard narrow-minded men who still assert that "women artists lack the essential sensitivity and understanding" necessary to make them valid contributors to the progress of art. Her work, both as composer and writer, have [sic] commanded respect

and admiration from men and women alike, musician and non-musician, and has placed her name upon the identical high level of stature already occupied by other distinguished artists of music.

Upon first entering her home in mid-upper Manhattan the visitor is immediately impressed by the enormous book shelves lined with books and music manuscripts that reach from floor to ceiling and seem to cover the entire living room. A grand piano occupies the center of the room and is stacked with music scores of all sizes and description. One has the impression of walking amidst a century of creative culture, as he strolls through the front-room, taking particular notice of the musical materials concentrated within arm's reach. Miss Bauer, who shares her abode with her sister Flora, is a charming and friendly woman in her sixties, with the vitality and energy comparable to a woman half her age. Here is no "problem-child" personality. Her gracious manner and healthy minded approach to her own creative work, and her warm-hearted smile and amiable manner have been especially receptive to the younger generation of composers and musicians who are constantly calling upon her for advice and encouragement....

In speaking of her career as teacher and lecturer, and the relative function of both, Miss Bauer said, "The real function of a teacher is not to force upon any student one's own ideas or methods, or type of work. The true function is to develop the student's own talent and help him to find himself and his individual style. To develop from inside out——not from outside in," is the way she puts it....

Speaking of music and women composers in general, Miss Bauer was very emphatic. "My early aspiration was not to listen to the sly remarks of intolerant men regarding women composers...that if given reasonable chance for development, an individual talent, regardless of sex, can progress and grow." In relation to her own music, Miss Bauer was quite specific and said, "I haven't any use for modernists who deny tradition and the things of the past, but I hope I am walking forward into the future. I have not used Indian music or jazz as a basis on which to write, and I do not know that anyone can say that my work is definitely American. I hope it is definitely a reflection of my own cultural background, environment and personality."[29]

All-Marion Bauer Town Hall Concert

The Phi Beta fraternity sponsored an all-Marion Bauer concert, which was held at Town Hall on 8 May 1951. Two pieces received their first performance: *Moods for Dance Interpretation*, opus 46 (piano and dancer, and later expanded and revised as a solo piano work, *Moods*) and *Trio Sonata II* (flute, cello, piano). The cover of *The Baton* was adorned with a picture of Marion along with a few measures from the manuscript of her new trio. The music of the trio has not been found, so *The Baton* cover serves only to whet the appetite for one of Marion's last chamber works. The others pieces on the program were representative of Marion's entire career.[30] Marion said the concert was one of the great events of her professional life.[31]

Olin Downes reviewed the concert in *The New York Times:* "It...may be said of [Bauer's compositions], that whatever their particular strength or weaknesses might prove to be, each one was concentrated and to the point. There is no padding in this music, no treading water, no waiting an appointed number of measures to introduce the second theme or its development. The music is prevailingly contrapuntal and dissonance is not absent. Yet the fundamental conception is melodic, the thinking clear and logical, the sentiment sincere and direct."[32]

Shortly after the concert, Marion wrote a letter of thanks to Aaron Copland for his contribution to the event, in which she remarked, "Can you imagine me as 'Prima Donna for a Day!'"[33] Her excitement, pride, and afterglow are palpable. A few weeks after the Town Hall concert, on 20 June 1951, Marion received an honorary Doctor of Music degree from the New York College of Music "for distinguished professional services and outstanding achievements in Music Education."[34]

Symphony No. 1

Her first major post-retirement musical event was supposed to be the November 1951 premiere performance of her *Symphony No. 1*, conducted by Howard Hanson at the Symposium of American Orchestral Music at the Eastman School of Music in Rochester, NY. It is a three-movement work, composed for a large orchestra. Marion specified that it is not programmatic. The first movement is in a free sonata form. The second movement is a scherzo, but the trio section is quite lyrical and slower in tempo. About the third movement, Marion wrote, "[It] is a Passacaglia which works up to a tremendous contrapuntal climax at the end. The heart of the symphony can be likened to modern organum, which is the use of thematic material in open fourths and fifths. The orchestral climax at the end is really quite ear-shattering in its aural proportions."[35]

Marion's description of the organum-like quintal harmony is a reference to the pervasive parallel motion; she also incorporates pantriadicism (consecutive unrelated triads). It is possible that her orchestration of *Sun Splendor* during the earlier 1940s rekindled her interest in quintal harmony. Unlike in her other orchestral works, there is a considerable variety of texture in this symphony: solo woodwind passages, string passages, brass interludes, and the use of the full orchestra. In the last movement begins with a distinct harmonic idea followed by a series of variations on that idea. Whether the last movement of Brahms's fourth symphony influenced her is not known, but the educated listener might reasonably suspect so.

Marion had three copyists create the orchestral parts for the performers from her full score. Unfortunately, according to her letter to Howard

Hanson, dated shortly before the symposium began, the copyists' work was abysmal: "There were literally hundreds of errors—notes mis-read, ties omitted, dynamics forgotten, even wrong instruments copied in the parts." She concluded the letter by saying, "That I am bitterly disappointed goes without saying."[36] She was unable to correct the orchestral parts in time for the work to be performed. In another letter, written a week later, Marion expressed "deep regret and embarrassment at having failed to complete the corrections."[37] She hoped that Howard Hanson might include her symphony in a later symposium, but he did not. Her symphony was never performed.[38] Although Marion does not tell us so, this surely must have been the profoundest disappointment of her career.

Other Post-Retirement Activities

Marion's retirement from NYU did not render her a woman of leisure. On the contrary, she composed, she taught part-time at The Juilliard School and New York College of Music, and she and Flora continued their work with *The Musical Leader*. An article in *The Musical Leader* recounted two months of Marion's retirement activities, which showed that her life was a whirlwind of activity, even without her NYU duties, and that much more of her energy was focused on getting her most recent compositions performed.[39]

Marion also collaborated with Ethel Peyser on an opera history book, *How Opera Grew*. It was finished shortly before Marion's death and published the next year, with Peyser's name listed as first author (which, frankly, seems ungenerous). Marion's archive at NYU contains notes and proposals for four more books: *Modern Creators of Music*, *Titans of Music*, *Some Social Aspects of Music*, and *Who Was Monteverdi?* Marion mentioned another book "in preparation" in 1951, entitled *Music is a Language*,[40] but no trace of it has been found. (Perhaps she subsequently changed the title, and it was one of the books previously mentioned.)

In mid-1953, Marion was "thrilled" to learn that the Composers' Forum wanted an all-Marion Bauer program: "I will mark down February 6 in red letters." She outlined her thoughts about which new pieces might be performed, wanting to include only one work from the Town Hall recital of 1951 (*Piano Trio No. 2*). The new works she proposed were her *Five Pieces for String Quartet*, opus 41[b] and her *Woodwind Quintet*, opus 48. In addition, she said, "I may have a new and short sonata for violin and piano that is well begun for Arved Kurtz, and I have been doing some songs, so I will have plenty of new things to choose from."[41] Although this impending program was not as lofty an affair as the Town Hall recital, it was clear that Marion looked forward to it enthusiastically; it gave her a goal to work toward and a deadline for her compositions that were in progress.

Just One

Sadly, the actual program was quite different than she had anticipated. Only three of her compositions were performed—*Piano Trio No. 2, Moods* for solo piano, and her older *Duo for Oboe and Clarinet*—and the rest of the program was works by another composer. Perhaps the reason that Marion's new works were not completed was Flora's deteriorating health. Flora died three days after the recital. Her obituary ended with, "Her sister is her only survivor."[42]

After Flora's death, Marion took over the duties for *The Musical Leader* that the three Bauer sisters had faithfully fulfilled for fifty-four years. After a few months, she happily handed the daily duties over to someone else,[43] although she continued contributing her "According to Marion Bauer" column, as well as "At the Metropolitan," and special articles.

A program of Marion's works was performed on WNYC radio in November 1954 by Carey Sparks, tenor, and Dorothy Eustis, piano.[44] Marion was the commentator for the program. Her song entitled "Here Alone, Unknown," with a text by Conrad Aiken (1889–1973), was one of the works presented. Although Marion's holograph of the work is undated, given the text she chose it is tempting to speculate that she composed the song shortly after Flora's death. Two other new songs that were performed on the program, "Dreams in the Dusk" and "From the Shore," have not been located.[45]

On 6 August 1955, Marion went to the MacDowell Colony for a special gathering of colonists. The next day she was back at Harrison and Margaret Potter's home in South Hadley, Massachusetts, where she was vacationing. There, she wrote her last known letter, to Marian MacDowell. It revealed that Marion was still mourning Flora's death from eighteen months earlier: "In spite of the enjoyment I got out of the entire experience, it made me feel sad too. My thoughts of Flora and the many happy years we had there with you and Nina Maud were quite overwhelming. But I have had to learn to make the happy memories outweigh the sorrowful ones.... I did so appreciate your last sweet letter. How well you understand what Flora's going meant to me."[46]

Marion Eugénie Bauer Dies

Three days later, on 9 August 1955, Marion Eugénie Bauer suffered a heart attack at the Potters' home, and died there in the arms of her longtime friend. Although her obituary in *The New York Times* stated, "She would have been 68 years old next Monday,"[47] she actually would have been seventy-three.

We know essentially nothing about Marion's religious beliefs during her adult life. (She may have had some interest in Christian Science, but that has not been confirmed.)[48] We do know that a rabbi officiated at her memorial service. The Kensico Cemetery in Valhalla, NY does have a Jewish section, but the Bauer sisters chose not to be buried in that area. Marion's ashes were placed in the same plot as Emilie Frances and Minnie. Flora and her husband rest beside them.[49] Marion's headstone boldly declares "1884" as her birth year.

The Bauer sisters' graves.[50]

Gustave Reese, who was a musicologist and a colleague of Marion's at NYU, spoke at her funeral. Among his most touching remarks are, "Marion Bauer was a person admirable in so many ways that those who knew her well and who will continue to remember her affectionately need never wonder what to praise, but only what to praise first." He went on to distinguish her as "the outstanding woman among American composers with what were then modern tendencies." He praised her for helping to build "receptive audiences for newer idioms and newer styles." He said her music was "characterized by craftsmanship, individuality, and elegance."[51]

The *Musical Courier* emphasized her impact on students, "Her name will be long cherished in the hearts of numerous young composers and artists whose way she lighted with her never-failing cheer and helpfulness.... A great lady and a great friend, the place she has left cannot be filled."[52]

Harold Schoenberg, a music critic for *The New York Times*, wrote a lengthy and elegant memorial, which extolled Marion's professional virtues and personal values. He said, "No more dedicated and unselfish person ever existed. Her pupils, among whom the writer was one, adored her." He concluded with, "Her pupils and friends will miss her. For she had the ability to draw out the best in them. Nobody was more of an appreciator, in the best sense of the word, than Marion Bauer."[53] Her many friends, colleagues, and students remembered her as a person who was warm and laughed easily, and who was compassionate and generous.[54]

In December 1955, the New York University-Washington Square College chorus opened their concert with Marion's elegant choral work *Death Spreads His Gentle Wings*.[55] She had composed the work in memory of the conductor, Walter Howe, but in the end, the composition commemorated the composer herself.

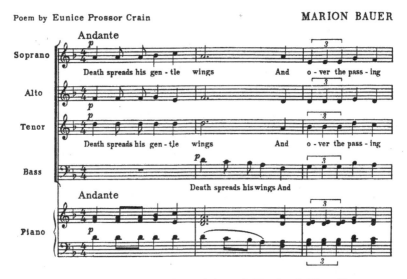

In memory of Walter Howe

Death Spreads His Gentle Wings

(for a cappella Chorus)

Poem by Eunice Prossor Crain   MARION BAUER

Opening measures of *Death Spreads His Gentle Wings*.[56]

---

1   American Music Center website, www.amc.net (accessed 20 April 2007).

2   The League of Composers concert in question occurred 26 Feb 1939. There are two differing accounts of this story. One is from Marion Bauer and Claire Reis, "Twenty-Five Years with the League of Composers," *MQ* 34/1 (Jan 1948): 1–14. The second account is in Claire Reis, *Composers, Conductors and Critics* (New

York: Oxford Univ. Press, 1955), 57. The confusion between the accounts was cleared up by this source: "Illness Brings Changes," ML 71/5 (11 Mar 1939), 11.

[3] Marion Bauer and Flora Bauer, published letter to Florence French, *ML* 71/13 (2 Aug 1939), 2.

[4] "A Message of Appreciation," ML 71/13 (Aug 1939), 2.

[5] The Mar 1940 issue.

[6] She also contributed seventy-five articles to Oscar Thompson's *International Cyclopedia of Music and Musicians* (1939), and was on the Board of Associates for that tome as well. For later editions she was an Associate Editor.

[7] Marion Bauer, *Musical Questions and Quizzes* (New York: G. P. Putnam's Sons, 1941), xi.

[8] G. F., "Marion Bauer's Concerto Played," *ML* 75/6 (June 1943), 21.

[9] She had orchestrated some works, such as her song "Orientale," but those holographs have not been found. Therefore, their instrumentations are unknown.

[10] An excellent recording is available: see Appendix 3 for details.

[11] It premiered 29 March 1941, though the holograph is undated. The style is consistent with other songs known to be composed around this time. The title on Marion's holograph is "Benediction."

[12] N. S., "Festival is Ended by Biblical Music," *NYT*, 30 Mar 1941, 46.

[13] Martha Furman Schleifer, e-mail message to author, 16 Feb 2008.

[14] More information about this composition is found in Appendix 1. Complete information is found at marionbauer.org.

[15] Marion Bauer to Ross Lee Finney, 1942, Ross Lee Finney, correspondence/box 1. Library of Congress, Washington, DC.

[16] "Marion Bauer's Choral Work Performed," *ML* 77/11 (Nov 1945), 6.

[17] The orchestral score is not in any of the usual repositories of Marion's works, nor is it in the Philadelphia Orchestra library or the Worcester Festival library.

[18] *NYT*, "Radio Programs of the Week," 16 Mar 1947, X10.

[19] "Marion Bauer's Compositions Heard," *ML* 79/4 (Apr 1947), 7. The review in the *New York Herald Tribune* by F. D. P. [Francis Perkins] was quoted in the *ML*.

[20] More information about this composition is found in Appendix 1. Complete information is found at marionbauer.org.

[21] Charles Mills, "Over the Air," *Modern Music 21/3* (Mar-Apr 1944): 191.

[22] "Marion Bauer on the Air," *ML* 75/3 (Mar 1943), 11.

[23] F. D. P. [Francis Perkins], "Stokowski Presents Work by Marion Bauer," *ML* 79/11 (Nov 1947), 2 and 8. The *Musical Leader* reprinted the review, but without original publication information.

[24] R. P. [Ross Parmenter?], "Bauer Work Presented," *NYT*, 26 Oct 1947, 42.

[25] The New York Philharmonic archive generously allows access, by appointment, to the archives. The recording is in excellent condition. Owing to union rules, the recording cannot be duplicated, even for educational purposes.

26 Fortunately, Nancy Thurmond Sutton engraved the score and conducted the piece, and has a photocopy of Bauer's holograph. Nancy Thurmond Sutton and Marion Bauer. 2000. Vol. I Sun splendor of Marion Bauer: a biographical, analytical and performance examination of Sun splendor, a tone poem for full orchestra composed by Marion Bauer, 1882-1955; Vol. II Sun splendor of Marion Bauer: a critical first performance edition. Thesis (D.M.A.)––University of California, Los Angeles, 2000. The orchestral parts used by the New York Philharmonic are in the Houghton Library at Harvard University (Moldenhauer Archive), Cambridge, MA.

27 Marion Bauer to H. R. Austin, 2 Feb 1951.

28 Jeannette L. Henn, editor, *The Baton* of the Phi Beta Fraternity 30/3 (Mar 1951): 1.

29 Bazelon, "Woman With a Symphony," in *The Baton* of the Phi Beta Fraternity 30/3 (Mar 1951): 4-7. Reproduced herein with the kind permission of Phi Beta.

30 Phi Beta Fraternity, concert program, "Phi Beta Fraternity presents a program devoted to the works of Marion Bauer," 8 May 1951, Town Hall, NY, NY.

31 *Goss, Modern Music-Makers, 136.*

32 Olin Downes, "Miss Bauer's Work Makes Up Concert," *NYT,* 9 May 1951, 41.

33 Marion Bauer to Aaron Copland, undated [May or June 1951], Aaron Copland Collection, correspondence 1911–1991, box/folder/246/27, Library of Congress, Washington, DC.

34 "N. Y. College of Music Honors Marion Bauer," *ML* 83/12 (Dec 1951), 5. The New York College of Music was incorporated into New York University in 1968.

35 Bazelon, "Woman With a Symphony," 7. In publicity materials Marion provided for the symposium, she said, "The first movement approaches sonata form but is more like a large prelude. The second movement, a scherzo in 2/4 time is interrupted by a slower pastoral mood with a return to the scherzo. The third movement is a free passacaglia or better still a chaconne which works up to a contrapuntal close." Marion Bauer to Alma Judd, 15 Oct 1951, Howard Hanson Papers/Symposium of American Orchestral Music Fall 1951/box 28/10, Sibley Music Library, Eastman School of Music, Rochester, NY.

36 Marion Bauer to Howard Hanson, 26 Oct 1951, Howard Hanson Papers/Symposium of American Orchestral Music Fall 1951/box 28/10, Sibley Music Library, Eastman School of Music, Rochester, NY.

37 Marion Bauer to Mary Louise Creegan, 4 Nov 1951, Howard Hanson Papers/Symposium of American Orchestral Music Fall 1951/box 28/10, Sibley Music Library, Eastman School of Music, Rochester, NY.

38 One hopes that she was able to have the NYU or Juilliard orchestra read through her symphony, but no evidence has been found.

39 "Marion Bauer's Activities," *ML* 85/3 (Mar 1953), 23.

40 Marion Bauer to Alma Judd, 15 Oct 1951, Howard Hanson Papers/Symposium of American Orchestral Music Fall 1951/box 28/10, Sibley Music Library, Eastman School of Music, Rochester, NY.

41 Marion Bauer to Peggy [Glanville-Hicks?], 1 June 1953, Composers Forum, letters, folder 299, New York Public Library for the Performing Arts, NY, NY.

42 *NYT*, "Mrs. R. A. Bernstein," 10 Feb 1954, 29.

43 Shirley Cash took over as New York Representative in September 1954.

44 *NYT*, "Radio Highlights of the Week," 7 Nov 1954, X15.

45 A holograph of a song entitled "Dusk" is extant, though undated. Its style suggests that it is an early work, so "Dreams in the Dusk" is probably a different song.

46 Marion Bauer to Marian MacDowell, 7 Aug 1955, Edward and Marian MacDowell Collection, papers of Marian Nevins MacDowell, box 42. Library of Congress, Washington, DC.

47 *NYT*, "Marion E. Bauer, Composer, is Dead," 11 Aug 1955, 21.

48 Marion's friend, Frederic Stoessel, said she was interested in Christian Science during the 1950s, but also referred to her as a "Jewish woman."

49 Uncas, section 184, plot 7758, grave 3.

50 Photograph by Robert Arnold Johnson.

51 Reese's remarks are quoted by Ethel Peyser in, "In Memory––Marion Bauer," in The Baton of the Phi Beta Fraternity 35/1 (Nov 1955): 5 and 8.

52 "Deceased," *MC* 152/3 (Sep 1955), 33–34.

53 H. C. S. [Harold Schoenberg], "Champion of American Composer," *NYT*, 14 Aug 1955, X7.

54 Fred Stoessel, "My Memories of Marion Bauer." (See Appendix 4.)

55 *NYT*, "Concert and Opera Programs for the Week," 11 Dec 1955, 158.

56 More information about this composition is found in Appendix 1. Complete information is found at marionbauer.org.

CHAPTER 9

POSTLUDE

W hy hasn't Marion Bauer's music been performed much since her death? The punchy answer is: because she was a woman composer. The real answer is more complicated and a catch-22. Music is an aural art, so performances of her music are necessary for it to become known and evaluated. Performances depend on the music being available, but almost all of her published music is not currently in print, nor is it likely to be reprinted until her music is known better. And why should a publisher take on by an unknown deceased composer whose music is rarely recorded, and is, therefore, less salable? To further complicate the matter, her manuscripts are not yet in public domain, and until recently there had been obstacles regarding her estate, so getting permission to copy manuscripts was difficult.

The first complete list of her works is included herein (see Appendix 1) and a detailed and annotated list of those works can be found at marionbauer. org. Having the annotated list of her works, which includes locations of her manuscripts, is a big step toward renewing performers' interest in her music: at least the music can now be easily found. "Sift the wheat from the chaff," Marion told us. That is what we should do with her music. Where do we start? In my opinion, the following works should be the first to be reprinted and recorded, because they are among her best: "Light" (song); "The Red Man's Requiem" (song); *Up the Ocklawaha* (violin and piano); "By the Indus" (song); *Three Impressions* (piano); "My Faun" (song); "Night in the Woods" (song); *From the New Hampshire Woods* (piano);

Six Preludes (piano); "A Fancy" (piano); *Duo for Oboe and Clarinet* (oboe and clarinet); *Piano Concerto* (piano and orchestra; also arranged for two pianos); "Swan" (song); "Harp" (song); *Death Spreads His Gentle Wings* (chorus); and "Here Alone" (song). Some of these works are available on two recent recordings: the first features the pianist Stephen Beus and the second is by the Ambache Chamber Orchestra and Ensemble. These recordings make a strong case that Marion's music is worthy of modern consideration.

Marion Bauer's music—and the music of literally thousands of other women composers—is too often dismissed because of the woefully mistaken assumption that the lack of its availability is an indicator of a lack of quality. To this must be added that some contemporary writers (who have the resources to know better) perpetuate myths, such as Norman Lebrecht's information about Marion, published in 1992: "Marion (Eugenie) Bauer. Author of romantic piano pieces [her style is not romantic] with flowery titles—*A Garden Is a Lovesome Thing* [this is not a piano piece], *From the New Hampshire Woods*, *Sun Splendour* [misspelled]...—and educational music books. She also composed an *American Youth* piano concerto (1943) and a cantata on *China* (1944) [this representation of her output is pitiful]. b. Walla Walla, Washington, US, 1897 [not even close to her birth year]."[1] Disgraceful.

Last Will and Testament

Marion's friend, Harrison Potter, was in charge of dispensing with Marion's most treasured possession: her music. He donated her holographs and printed music to the New York Public Library for the Performing Arts, the Library of Congress, and Mount Holyoke College. Some of her manuscripts are missing, including *Sun Splendor* for solo piano and *Sonata for Violin and Piano in G Minor*, which, gauging from reviews, may have been among her more important works.

Regarding the rest of her estate, it was valued at about $50,000 at the time of her death (about $425,000 in 2012 dollars). Twenty percent was split among various organizations and people. Forty percent went to

Harrison Potter and his wife. That bequest makes sense: the Potters were long-time friends with Marion, and Harrison Potter had championed her piano music on his recitals. The remaining forty percent went to Olive G. Taylor, whose address was in New York City. It is almost certain that she was the same Olive Taylor who joined *The Musical Leader* staff in 1932, and who was "associated with...Marion and Flora Bauer."[2] Census records, newspapers, and phone books reveal that she may have been Olive Ulrich, who "studied music abroad and acted small parts in 'The Opera Ball' in 1912...[and] 'My Best Girl.'" She married George H. Taylor in 1913.[3] George Taylor probably deceased as of 1931, and Olive G. (Ulrich) Taylor died in 1977.[4] Why did Marion leave so much money to her? Was she a lover? A close friend? Both? The absence of a single clue signals that we may never know.

Personal Anecdotes

Coincidences and eerie events have accompanied my quest for information about Marion and Emilie Frances. The first time I saw Marion Bauer's name was in 1990 (my interest in Emilie Frances came later). I read a brief paragraph about Marion (that I later came to know was filled with errors). Three facts caught my eye: that she was born on August 15 (that's my birthday too), that she was born in Walla Walla (where, at that time, I had taught ten years without hearing her name), and that Stokowski had conducted one of her works. Why hadn't I heard of her?

I asked the Chair of the Music Department at New York University whether any of Marion's colleagues were still around. I was told that there was one, Martin Bernstein, and that he was in his late eighties. Bernstein and I had a bad telephone connection and he may have been a little hard of hearing as well——it was one of those difficult conversations where I felt like I was shouting into the phone. Still, he was very helpful. Of course, I had initially introduced myself and mentioned that I taught at Whitman College, but about thirty minutes into the conversation he said, "You're in Walla Walla, right? Have you ever heard of Whitman College?" I explained again that I taught there. He said, "My nephew is President of Whitman

College." Sure enough, I was speaking to President Maxwell's uncle. (David Maxwell was President of Whitman College from 1989–1993.)

Graveyard Stories

Jacques Bauer, his brother, Robert, and two Bauer children who died very young, are buried in Walla Walla. When I first saw the Bauer gravesite, all of the headstones and footstones were askew, suffering from over a century of wear and tear and neglect. It was impossible to tell where the headstones and footstones really belonged. The headstones bear the first names of the deceased, and the footstones say "Bauer." They are small, half-moon- shaped marble markers with two holes drilled in the bottom of each. Ideally, the marble stones should sit on top of flat rocks implanted in the ground. Those flat rocks also have holes drilled in them. Little brass rods should have been inserted into the sets of holes, loosely connecting the half-moon headstones to the foundation stones. But no foundation stones were to be seen. I figured they must be under a few inches of dirt, but I also thought that it might be considered untoward for a college professor to be seen digging in the local graveyard. Not to be deterred from such an important task, I waited until dusk and went back to the graveyard with a flashlight, trowel, ruler, paper, and pencil. On my hands and knees I gently tapped the tip of my trowel into the ground around the gravestones. "Clink" was the sound of my trowel locating a foundation stone under a few inches of dirt. Clink ..... clink ..... clink ..... clink ..... clink, and within a few minutes I had located and uncovered all of them. The distances between the two holes in each foundation stone were unique, quickly revealing where each headstone and footstone belonged. I drew a map as night descended on the graveyard. The next day, I approached the woman who oversaw the cemetery, and told her what I had discovered, and said that I wanted to straighten out the Bauer site. "Oh! You must be a relative," she said, smiling. I was honest, and said I wasn't. (I learned from these experiences to always lie when asked if I was related to the Bauers.) She didn't say anything, but her expression changed, and there was no doubt in my mind that she was thinking, "Who is this nut, and why is she digging in my graveyard?" I quickly explained about Marion Bauer and her family. Her excitement about the Bauer story motivated her to ask for a copy of Jacques's obituary for their local history collection. Then she found a company to donate the brass rods to reconnect the marble stones to their foundations. She procured a hacksaw and made the brass rods just the right length, as I looked on with gratitude. I still visit the graves often.

A time came during my research when I wanted to know where Marion was buried. I didn't yet have Marion's will (which specified her burial plans), so I called the Frank Campbell Funeral Home in New York City, because I had noticed in one of Marion's obituaries that they had handled her funeral. When I told them what I wanted, I heard what I thought was a soft sigh over the telephone, and was told that those records were in the basement, that it would take some time to find them, and that I should call back in a few weeks. Over the following months, I did call them a few times, but they had not yet had time to look for the records. A year later, unbeknownst to the funeral home, my husband and I went to New York City to hear some concerts. We were sitting in a coffee shop near Lincoln Center, and my husband said, "Let's check out the Frank Campbell funeral home." I hesitated–I was discouraged. He insisted. As we walked in, we were greeted by a man in a very black suit, looking quite solemn, who asked, "May I help you?" I told him what I wanted, that I had been in contact over the last year, and that we thought we'd just drop in. He sought his assistant, with whom I had the previous telephone conversations. He returned, now looking a little bemused. As it turned out, just as we were walking in the front door, his assistant had been looking for the Bauer records in the basement. But she had an asthma attack from all the dust and had to go to the pharmacy. So the kind gentleman descended into the basement, and soon reappeared with the burial records in hand, his suit now a bit dusty.

We were unable to visit the graves on that trip, which was disappointing. Soon after we arrived back in Walla Walla, however, I received a phone call from a former student who wanted to update me on her address. She had just moved to Valhalla, New York. "Peggy, get your camera and go to the graveyard," I said. A week later, I saw pictures of the sisters' graves.

During the summer of 2007, my husband and I made a pilgrimage there. The Bauer sisters rest on a serene hillside.

---

1   Norman Lebrecht, *The Companion to Twentieth Century Music* (New York: Simon and Schuster, 1992), 22.

2   "Olive Taylor Joins Our Staff," *ML* 62/9 (3 Mar 1932), 3.

3   *NYT*, "G. H. Taylor Weds Abroad," 12 Sep 1913: 8.

4   *NYT*, "Deaths," 8 Feb 1977

APPENDIX 1

Marion Bauer: Compositions

A detailed and annotated list is found at marionbauer.org

Marion Bauer's compositions are listed below in chronological order, with preference given to known dates of composition, premiere dates, copyright dates, and/or opus numbers. Works with inclusive dates, such as 1941–1942, are placed under the later date (in this case, 1942). The placement of compositions with no known dates is determined by other means, such as style, dates of advertisements, references to the works in dated correspondence, the brand of manuscript paper on which they are written, and so forth. When a composition has more than one date (for example, if Marion had revised it), it is placed by the most recent date. Marion was a woman of many gifts, but accuracy with numbers apparently wasn't among them. She occasionally claims a work was composed in a particular year, only to be contradicted by her own dated correspondence. Dates of her compositions are often incorrect in print sources––even modern ones. So much misinformation abounds that no effort has been made to enumerate those mistakes here, only to provide correct information.

She assigned opus numbers only to larger works, with a few exceptions. There are no known works designated opus 1, 2, 3, 4, 7, 9, 11, 13, 23, or 28 (although presumably her first two published works, "Arabesque" and "Elegie," are opuses 1 and 2). Her opus numbers are often unreliable indicators of chronology, and are used in that way here only when no other source of dating is found. Duplicate opus numbers appear on a few musically unrelated works: opus 21, 22, 29, 33, 39#2, and 48.

Marion and/or her publishers occasionally changed the title of a work before its publication. Other titles have been misquoted, misspelled, and/or otherwise altered in print sources from the 1920s onward. All titles known to be associated with a work are listed here; the primary title is what is found on the music itself, unless otherwise indicated.

Marion Bauer's works are listed by title, and alternate title(s) (if applicable); opus (if applicable); medium; and date. Exhaustive details about the works, their texts (when applicable), revisions, duplicate opus numbers, publications, and so forth, can be found at marionbauer.org.

Brackets indicate editorial comments. Parenthetic phrases in titles are original to Marion's manuscripts and published music.

Spurious Works:

Der 28. Psalm. Wenn ich Rufe an Dich, Herr, mein Gott; published under "M. Bauer." This work is often attributed to Marion Bauer. It is by Moritz Bauer (1875–1932).

Sieben Lieder; published under "M. Bauer." These songs are often attributed to Marion Bauer. They are by Moritz Bauer (1875–1932).

Compositions:

1. Arabesque; piano; 1904.
2. Elegie; piano; 1904.
3. Canzonetta in G; violin/piano; 1904–1905?
4. Light; voice/piano; 1907-1908?
5. Bacchanale; voice/piano; 1909–1910?
6. Coyote Song; voice/piano; 1909–1910?
7. Echo; voice/piano; 1909–1910?
8. Nocturne; voice/piano; 1909–1910?
9. Out of the West [Suite]; piano; 1910?
10. Melancolié; voice/piano; 1910 or 1911?
11. Star Trysts [a.k.a. The Dream Stream]; voice/piano; 1910–1911?
12. The Last Word; voice/piano; 1911?

13. The Mill-Wheel [a.k.a. Das Mühlenrad]; voice/piano; 1911?
14. Over the Hills; voice/piano; 1911?
15. The Red Man's Requiem; voice/piano; 1911?
16. Send Me a Dream (Intuition); voice/piano; 1911?
17. Song of the Earth; voice/piano; 1911?
18. Were I a Bird On Wing [a.k.a. Wenn ich ein Waldvöglein wär]; voice/piano; 1911.
19. The Desert; recitation/piano; 1911-1912?
20. The Enfifa River; recitation/piano; 1911-1912?
21. A Lament; recitation/piano; 1911-1912?
22. Midsummer Days; recitation/piano; 1911-1912?
23. O That We Two Were Maying; recitation/piano; 1911-1912?
24. Prospice; recitation/piano; 1911-1912?
25. The Relief of Lucknow: An Incident of the Sepoy Mutiny; recitation/piano; 1911-1912?
26. Sleep; recitation/piano; 1911-1912?
27. Song from "A Blot on the 'Scutcheon"; recitation/piano; 1911-1912?
28. Suppliant; recitation/piano; 1911-1912?
29. Young Endymion; recitation/piano; 1911-1912?
30. The Forsaken Merman (A Melodrama); recitation/piano; 1912.
31. The Shadows; voice/piano; 1912?
32. [Untitled; text begins with Weavers, weaving at break of day]; voice/piano; 1912?
33. Up the Ocklawaha, op. 6; violin/piano; 1912.
34. Fair Daffodils; women's chorus/piano; 1913?
35. In the Country: Four Little Piano Pieces, op. 5; piano [pedagogical]; 1913.
36. Only of Thee and Me; voice/piano; 1913?
37. Danse Lente; piano; 1914?
38. A Little Lane [a.k.a. A Little Lane Mid Shade and Sun]; voice/piano; 1914.
39. The Moonlight is a Silver Sea—version 1; voice/piano; 1914?
40. Phillis [a.k.a. Phyllis]; voice/piano; 1914.
41. Youth Comes Dancing O'er the Meadows [a.k.a. Spring Fantasy]; voice/piano; 1914.

42. The Lay of the Four Winds [a.k.a. The Winds], op. 8; men's chorus/piano; 1914–1915.
43. The Linnet is Tuning Her Flute; voice/piano; 1914–1915.
44. The Willow and the River; voice/piano; 1914–1915?
45. Lad and Lass; voice/piano; 1915?
46. The Minstrel of Romance; voice/piano; 1915–1916.
47. Orientale [a.k.a. Fair Goes the Dancing; a.k.a. Threads of Brass?]; voice/piano; 1915–1916.
48. Das Erdenlied; voice/piano; 1912; revised, 1916.
49. By the Indus; voice/piano; 1916.
50. Little Sleeper; voice/piano; 1916.
51. The Malay to his Master; voice/piano; 1916?
52. Three Impressions, op. 10; piano; 1917.
53. From Hills of Dream [a.k.a. Fairy Lullaby]; voice/piano; 1917–1918.
54. The Epitaph of a Butterfly [a.k.a. The Last Butterfly]; voice/piano; 1918?
55. Night in the Woods; voice/piano; 1918.
56. A Parable (The Blade of Grass); voice/piano; 1918.
57. Roses Breathe in the Night; voice/piano; 1918?
58. The Driftwood Fire; voice/piano; 1919.
59. Gold of the Day and Night [a.k.a. My Song of You]; voice/piano; 1919.
60. The Moonlight is a Silver Sea–version 2; voice/piano; 1919?
61. My Faun; voice/piano; 1919.
62. Thoughts; voice/piano; 1919.
63. Allegretto Giocoso; 11 instruments [probably woodwinds and strings]; 1920.
64. From The New Hampshire Woods: A Suite of Three Pieces, op. 12; piano; 1920.
65. Sonata [No. 1] for Violin and Piano in G Minor, op. 14; violin/piano; 1919–1921.
66. Cortège; unknown; 1920–1921?
67. Serentina; chamber orchestra (woodwinds and strings); 1921–1922?
68. Six Preludes, op. 15; piano; 1921–1922.
69. Three Preludettes; piano; 1921–1922.
70. Cornflowers; piano; 1922?

71. Four Poems, op. 16; voice/piano; 1922.

72. Goldenrod; piano; 1922?

73. Introspection [a.k.a. Quietude], op. 17 #1; piano; 1924.

74. Turbulence, op. 17 #2; piano; 1924.

75. Fantasia Quasi Una Sonata [a.k.a. Sonata No. 2 for Violin and Piano], op. 18; violin/piano; 1924–1925.

76. A Fancy [a.k.a. Fairy Tale], op. 21 #1; piano; 1925?

77. Sun Splendor, op. 19[a]; piano; 1926.

78. String Quartet, op. 20; string quartet; 1925–1927.

79. [Untitled; Alice in Wonderland song cycle], op. 26; voice/piano; 1928.

80. [Untitled; The Lizards Scamper]; voice/piano; 1928?

81. Prometheus Bound [music for a play]; 2 flutes/2 piano; 1929.

82. Three Noëls (Tryste Nöel) [a.k.a. Three Christmas Carols], op. 22; women's chorus, a cappella; 1929.

83. Black-eyed Susan, Blue-eyed Grass; 2 v (both treble); 1930?

84. Four Piano Pieces, op. 21; piano; 1930.

85. If; 2 treble voices; 1930?

86. If I Were a Tree; 3 treble voices; 1930?

87. A Laugh is Just Like Sunshine; 3 v (all treble); 1930?

88. The Night Will Never Stay; 2 v (both treble); 1930?

89. An Open Secret; 3 v (all treble); 1930?

90. Sun Splendor; Op. 19[b]; 2 piano; 1930.

91. Here at High Morning, op. 27; male chorus, a cappella; 1931.

92. When the Shy Star Goes Forth; voice/piano; 1931.

93. Duo for Oboe and Clarinet [a.k.a. Suite for Oboe and Clarinet], op. 25: oboe/clarinet; 1932.

94. Orientale; voice/orchestra; 1932.

95. To Losers, op. 33 #2 voice/piano; 1932.

96. An Apple Orchard in the Spring; voice/piano?; 1933.

97. Faun Song; alto/chamber orchestra; 1933.

98. Rainbow and Flame; voice/piano; 1934.

99. Dance Sonata, op. 24; piano; 1931–1935.

100. Sonata for Viola (or Clarinet) and Piano, op. 22; viola or clarinet/piano; 1932 or 1935.

101. Four Songs with String Quartet [a.k.a. Suite for Soprano and String Quartet; a.k.a. Four Songs for Soprano and String Quartet], op. 30; soprano/string quartet; 1933–1936.

102. Five Greek Lyrics for flute alone [a.k.a. Forgotten Modes: Five Pieces for Flute (Alone)], op. 29; flute; 1936.

103. Thumb Box Sketches, op. 29; piano; 1936-1937.

104. Pan and Syrinx (a choreographic sketch), op. 31; flute/oboe/clarinet/string quartet/piano/percussion; 1937.

105. A Garden is a Lovesome Thing, op. 28; six-part mixed chorus; 1938.

106. The Thinker, op. 35; mixed chorus; 1938.

107. Sonatina for Oboe and Piano, op. 32a; oboe/piano; 1938–1939.

108. Concertino for Oboe, Clarinet, and String Quartet, op. 32[b]; 1939 or 1940.

109. Symphonic Suite for String Orchestra, op. 33; string orchestra; 1940.

110. Benediction [a.k.a. Priestly Benediction?]; voice/piano or organ; 1941?

111. The Harp; voice/piano; 1942.

112. Piano Concerto, "American Youth," op. 36; piano/orchestra or 2 piano; 1942.

113. With Liberty and Justice for All; voice/piano; 1942?

114. Wood Song of Triboulet; voice/piano; 1942?

115. Aquarelle [No. 1], op. 39 #1; piano; 1943.

116. The Last Frontier [a.k.a. Aquarelle No. 3?], op. 39 #2; piano; 1943?

117. A Letter; voice/piano; 1943?

118. Songs in the Night; voice/piano; 1943.

119. China, op. 38; SATB chorus/piano or orchestra; 1942–1944.

120. Trio Sonata No. 1, op. 40; flute/cello/piano; 1944.

121. Aquarelle No. 2, op. 39 #2; piano; 1945.

122. Aquarelle No. 3?, op. 39 #3; piano; 1945?

123. Sun Splendor: symphonic poem for orchestra; Op. 19[c]; orchestra; 1934–1946.

124. Patterns, op. 41; piano; 1946.

125. At the New Year, op. 42; SATB chorus/piano; 1947.

126. Dusk; voice/piano; 1947?
127. Night Etching; soprano/tenor/piano; 1947.
128. Prelude and Fugue for flute and piano; Op. 43[a]; flute/piano; 1947.
129. Song of the Wanderer [canon]; 3 voices; 1947.
130. Swan; voice/piano; 1947.
131. Aquarelle [No. 2] for chamber ensemble, op. 39 #2[b]; double woodwind quintet plus 2 string basses; 1948.
132. A New Solfeggietto (after C.P.E. Bach); piano; 1948.
133. Parade; piano; 1948.
134. Patterns [a.k.a. Paterns], op. 41[b] #2; double woodwind quintet plus string bass; 1948.
135. Prelude and Fugue for flute and string orchestra, op. 43[b]; flute/string orchestra; 1948.
136. Spring Day; piano; 1948.
137. Tumbling Tommy; piano; 1948.
138. Five Pieces for String Quartet, op. 41[c]; string quartet; 1946–1949.
139. Death Spreads His Gentle Wings; SATB chorus, a cappella; 1949.
140. Symphony No. 1, op. 45; orchestra; 1947–1950.
141. Anagrams, op. 48; piano; 1950.
142. Moods for Dance Interpretation, op. 46[a]; dancer/piano; 1950.
143. Meditation and Toccata; organ; 1951.
144. Trio Sonata No. 2, op. 47; flute/cello/piano; 1951.
145. Summertime Suite: 8 Pieces for Piano; piano; 1922–1952.
146. Playing Fireman; voice/piano; 1952?
147. Quintet for Woodwinds, op. 48; woodwind quintet; 1952?
148. A Foreigner Comes to Earth on Boston Common (Cantata), op. 49; mixed chorus/tenor solo/soprano solo/piano; 1951–1953.
149. April Morning; recitation/piano; 1953.
150. Eight Diversions from a Composer's Notebook; piano; 1953.
151. The Seven Candles; 3-part women's chorus; 1953?
152. Moods [a.k.a. Four Moods], op. 46[b]; piano; 1950–1954.
153. Dreams in the Dusk; voice/piano; 1953–1954?
154. From the Shore; voice/piano; 1953–1954?

155. [Sonata No. 3]; violin/piano; 1953–1954.
156. Here Alone, Unknown; voice/piano; 1954?
157. [Untitled: Five (?) pieces for piano, four-hands (?) or two pianos; pedagogical]; 1955?
158. [Ten pedagogical piano pieces]: The Spinning Wheel, Will O'the Wisp, Spring Rounds, Teasing, Irish Lament, Johnny-Jump-Ups, Gong Song, Dance Tune, Indian Ponies, Birds in Flight; piano [pedagogical]; 1955?
159. Sketches. Numerous incomplete sketches located at the New York Public Library for the Performing Arts.

Compositions–Arrangements

160. [Eskimo Songs]; voice/piano or string quartet; 1926.
161. Six Easy Fugues [a.k.a. Six Little Fugues] by G. F. Handel, edited/arr. by Marion Bauer; piano; 1940.
162. Six Little Fugues by G. F. Handel, edited/arranged by Marion Bauer; none; woodwind quintet; 1948.
163. Ein ungefärbt Gemüthe. Transcription of chorale from Cantata No. 24 by J. S. Bach; piano; 1950?
164. Ertödt uns durch dein Güte. Transcription of choral prelude from Cantata No. 22 by J. S. Bach; piano; 1950?
165. Sheep May Safely Graze. Transcription from Cantata No. 208 by J. S. Bach; piano; 1950?
166. Classics as Duets I; piano, 4 hands [pedagogical]; 1955?
167. Classics as Duets II; piano, 4 hands [pedagogical]; 1955?

APPENDIX 2

Emilie Frances Bauer: Compositions

A detailed and annotated list is found at marionbauer.org

Some were published under her pen name "Francisco di Nogero"

Emilie Frances Bauer's works are listed by title, and alternate title(s) (if applicable); opus (if applicable); medium; date of composition or publication. Many more details about the works, their texts (when applicable), publications, and so forth, can be found at marionbauer.org.

1. My Pets' Hush-a-bye (Slumber Song), op. 1?; 1884.
2. Murmurings from Venice (Barcarolle), op. 2; piano; 1884.
3. Moonlight on the Willamette (Waltzes), op. 3; piano; 1885.
4. My Love is a Muleteer / El Arriero [Francisco di Nogero]; voice/piano, & arr. for quartet (SATBar) and duet; 1916.
5. A Sevilla Love Song / Canción Sevillana [Francisco di Nogero]; voice/piano; 1916.
6. Our Flag in France: Here's to "Old Glory" and "Vive le Tricolor"; voice/piano & voice/orchestra or band; 1917.
7. A Spanish Knight [a.k.a. The Spanish Knight] [Francisco di Nogero]; voice/piano; 1918.
8. All Aboard the Slumber-Boat; voice/piano; unknown; 1918.
9. Tanguedilla [Tanguedia?]; unknown; unknown.
10. La Gitanina (From Roumanian Fields) [Francisco di Nogero]; voice/piano; 1919.
11. The Shadowy Garden [Francisco di Nogero]; voice/piano; 1921.
12. Neither Spirit nor Bird; voice/piano; 1921.
13. The Lost Lagoon; voice/piano; 1921.

APPENDIX 3

Discography

Recordings of compositions by the Bauer sisters

MARION BAUER'S COMPOSITIONS:

1. Title: America Virtuosa – Tribute to Maud Powell; Rachel Barton Pine, violin & Matthew Hagle, piano; compositions: *Up the Ocklawaha*, op. 6; Cedille Records 97, 2007.
2. Title: Excursions – Piano Music of Barber and Bauer; Stephen Beus, piano; compositions: *Three Impressions,* op. 10; *Six Preludes,* op. 15; "Pine-Trees" from *In the New Hampshire Woods,* op. 12 #3; Endeavour Classics 1017, 2006.
3. Title: American Classics – Marion Bauer; Ambache Chamber Ensemble and Chamber Orchestra; compositions: *Concerto for Piano,* "American Youth," op. 36; *Concertino for Oboe, Clarinet, and Strings,* op. 32b; *A Lament on an African Theme,* op. 20a (slow movement of Bauer's string quartet, op. 20, arr. for string orchestra by Martin Bernstein); *Symphonic Suite for String Orchestra,* op. 33 [recording says "opus 34" which is incorrect]; *Duo for Oboe and Clarinet,* op. 25; *Trio Sonata #1* (fl, cello, piano), op. 40; Naxos 8559253, 2005.
4. Title: Treasures. Little Known Songs by Women Composers; Linda Dykstra, soprano; Joan Conway, piano; compositions: "My Faun" and "How Doth the Little Crocodile" (songs); Spera, 2002.
5. Title: American Music for Violin and Piano; Elizabeth Reed Smith, violin; Leslie Petteys, piano; compositions: *Up the Ocklawaha,* op. 6; Albany Records 652, 2004.

6. Title: Marion Bauer; Virginia Eskin, piano, Irina Muresanu, violin, Deborah Boldin, flute; compositions: *Prelude and Fugue for Flute and Piano*, op. 43[a]; *Fantasia Quasi Una Sonata* for Violin and Piano, op. 18; *Six Preludes* for piano, op. 15; *Aquarelle*, op. 39 no 1 (piano); *Four Piano Pieces*, op. 21 #1 "Fancy"; *Dance Sonata* for piano, op. 24; Albany 465, 2001. [The information regarding "Fancy" on the CD is incorrect. Bauer has 2 works designated as op. 21 #1. This work, "A Fancy," is one of them, but is not the first movement of *Four Piano Pieces*, which is entitled "Chromaticon."]

7. Title: Bauer, Seeger: Chamber Music; Virginia Eskin, piano, Arnold Steinhardt, viola; compositions: *From the New Hampshire Woods*, opus 12 #1-3 (piano); *Turbulence*, op. 17 #2 (piano); *Sonata for Viola (or Clarinet) and Piano*, op. 22; *Four Piano Pieces*, op. 21 #1-4; Albany 297, 1998.

8. Title: Donne e Doni [II]; Susan Pickett, violin, Debra Richter, piano, Sonja Gourley, soprano; compositions: "Light"; "Nocturne"; "The Red Man's Requiem"; "Night in the Woods"; "Roses Breathe in the Night" (all are songs for voice and piano); private release, 1997.

9. Title: Women's Voices. Five Centuries of Song; Neva Pilgrim, soprano & Steven Heyman, piano; compositions: "I Love the Night" (song); Leonarda 338, 1997.

10. Title: Donne e Doni [I]; Susan Pickett, violin, Debra Richter [Bakland], piano, Sonja Gourley, soprano; compositions: *Up the Ocklawaha*, op. 6; private release, 1994.

11. Title: Four American Women; Virginia Eskin, piano; compositions: *From the New Hampshire Woods*, op. 12 #1-3; *Turbulence*, op. 17 #2; Northeastern Records 204/33 rpm recording and Sine Qua Non / cassette, 1981/1983.

12. Title: Piano Music, Virginia Eskin, piano; compositions: *Four Piano Pieces*, op. 21 #1-4; MHS 4236 / 33 rpm recording, 1980.

13. Title: Douglas Moore, Marion Bauer; Oslo Philharmonic; Charles Adler, conductor; compositions: *Symphonic Suite*, op. 33; *Prelude and Fugue for Flute and Orchestra*, op. 43[b]; CRI American Masters, CD 714, 1956 (33 rpm recording), 1996 (CD).

14. Title: Dorothy Eustis Plays Bach, Father and Son; Dorothy Eustis, piano; compositions: "Sheep may safely graze," from Cantata 208, J. S. Bach, arr. by Marion Bauer; unknown label (33 rpm recording), 1950.
15. Title: Piano Music by American Composers; Jeanne Behrend, piano; compositions: "White Birches," op. 12 #1 from *From the New Hampshire Woods*; RCA Victor (78 rpm recording), 1941.

EMILIE FRANCES BAUER'S COMPOSITIONS (Nom de plume: Francisco di Nogero):

1. Title: Ma little sunflow'r, good-night; Rosalie Miller, soprano, with orchestra [side B]; compositions: "My Love is a Muleteer" (sung in English); Pathé Frères 22327 (78 rpm recording), 1920.
2. Title: Ay, ay, ay! Vidalita Argentina; José Mardones, bass, with orchestra; compositions: "El arriero" ["My Love is a Muleteer"] (sung in Spanish); Columbia A3309 (78 rpm recording), 1920.

Appendix 4

Remembering

Fredric Stoessel and William Shank graciously contributed their memories of Marion:

My Memories of Marion Bauer
Fredric Stoessel
7 August 2006

The late Marion Bauer was my teacher and my close friend. She had been a family friend for years and I have childhood memories of her sitting in an armchair on the platform of the Chautauqua N.Y. amphitheatre while my father, the late Albert Stoessel, rehearsed one of her compositions. He thought highly of her as a composer and a musician.

Later, when Marion retired, and I graduated from N. Y. U., we became close friends––more like brother and older sister than teacher and pupil.

My father passed away in 1943. My mother and I moved to #1 West 72nd Street, the old Dakota Apartments. Marion lived a block away on West 73rd Street between Columbus and Amsterdam. Her sister, Flora, whom we called Floppy for some unknown reason, lived with her. Marion often came to our apartment because she and my mother were on the Board of Directors of the Society for the Publication of American Music (SPAM), which they often referred to as the Society for the Prevention of American Music.

I am not able to discuss Marion's music because I know little of it. I can discuss her as a beloved friend whom I miss to this day. She was Jewish and like most Jewish women was warm and outgoing. She laughed easily. Like many Jews she had a deep sense of spirituality, which came out in a certain tenderness in her compositions. Later she became interested in Christian Science. I was then emerging from the chaos of the Korean War in which I served as a LTjg in the Navy. Our conversations were over Biblical and metaphysical matters in which she was well versed. Often I would drive her to church services.

Directly after graduation I was recalled to Korea. We corresponded heavily mainly about the spiritual meaning of war and the reconstruction possibilities. There was a market just outside of the gate at Yokosuka called "Gyp Joint Alley" where one could purchase all sorts of gifts. I recall buying a tea set made of wood and sending it to her.

Later, when I returned, I would drive her to Peterborough, N. H. in early June where she spent a month composing at the MacDowell Colony. She brought her Jamaican maid, Ella, with her who was afraid to go in restaurants because of her color. So I would buy sandwiches and we could eat them in the car.

Returning to my N. Y. U. days, I had the feeling Marion did not like teaching Harmony I and II and would have preferred to teach advanced composition. Most of her pupils were jazz musicians who were adept on an instrument but lacked theory and musical development such as counterpoint and fugue. Many of her pupils went next door to study with Dr. Joseph Shillinger whose electronic theories enabled them to arrange and compose within a few months––an anathema to classical musicians.

Marion asked me to handle her finances, but I turned this one down. I was not trained in finances and did not want the responsibility involved. I gathered they were not massive. A friend, named Jesse, whose last name evades me, served in this capacity.

Marion died in the arms of our mutual friend, Harrison Potter, a pianist who taught at Mount Holyoke.

*

Remembering Marion Bauer
William Shank
Professor Emeritus, City University of New York,
Graduate School and University Center,
Music Librarian (retired).
18 July 2006

I was a student at N. Y. U. 1945–49 and also in the Graduate School 1949–52. Marion Bauer was my teacher and mentor. She took a genuine interest in my studies and my career development. I remember going to concerts of the League of Composers and ISCM; Marion Bauer was always there, always encouraging young composers and performers. Her enthusiasm was contagious; if there was a fault, it may have been that she, so far as I know, never gave a bad review. If a work was over-long and tedious, she would say, "It could use judicious pruning," always kind, considerate, encouraging.

I came to study music midway in my college career. I knew it was too late to develop into any kind of musician, but I was seriously taking every music course I could qualify for, same time drinking in the rich diet of music in New York–– concerts, opera, etc. I spent countless hours at the New York Public Library reading *The Musical Quarterly*, every article, every issue, as well as many, many books. At one time I told Miss Bauer that I was in a quandary about what to do career-wise. She suggested that there might be an opportunity in criticism and asked if I would like to be her assistant at The Musical Leader, where she was New York editor. There was no pay, but the experience was great and I got to hear countless concerts. I remember Arthur Berger telling me how lucky I was to get started there; he said many would pay for the chance. Another student at N. Y. U. wrote for her. Jay Smolens, who later changed his name to Jay S. Harrison and became Music Editor of the *N.Y. Herald Tribune*. Harold Schonberg was once her student. Seymour Solomon, the founder of Vanguard Records, was in our "Music Aesthetics and Criticism" class.

At one time, I think in 1947, she told me she had been commissioned to write a choral work based on the various seasons, would I know any poems that might be of interest. After some thought I suggested Kenneth Patchen's "At the New Year" from his *First Will and Testament*. She set the poem for chorus SATB and piano and it was performed at The New York Times Hall. Patchen was a friend of mine and I recall his getting a request for permission. I think the fee was $25. Miss Bauer gave me an inscribed copy of the score in appreciation. I had thought that Kenneth would be pleased that his poem was set to music but I think he was actually annoyed. He felt that the poem was a complete piece by itself and that any additions or modifications would diminish the work.

I didn't get into criticism although I did many articles and reviews for *Opera News, Library Journal, Musical Leader, Fanfare*, etc.

Marion Bauer wore an engagement ring; the rumor I heard was that it was for an engagement to Charles Tomlinson

Griffes. I don't know if there is any truth to that and do not recall her referring to it in her article in *The Musical Quarterly*.

I became a music librarian and retired from the CUNY Graduate School in 1991. I don't think any of us at N. Y. U. had any idea of whom we were studying with and the impact she would have on our lives. I was at Roosevelt University in 1955 when I heard the sad news that Marion Bauer had died.

*

Not everyone held Marion in high esteem. In *Talking Music* by William Duckworth, Milton Babbitt (1916-2011) recounted:

Duckworth: How did you get [to] New York University?

Babbitt: I read this book by Marion Bauer called *Twentieth Century Music*. That was one of the great turning points. Here was a book about twentieth-century music in which there were musical examples that I could sit down and play, or at least look at. And she knew about Schoenberg.... And I thought, "this is where I have to be," so I went to Washington Square College/NYU and had the happiest days of my life....

Duckworth: What was Marion Bauer like?

Babbitt: Marion Bauer was one of the dearest, most wonderful creatures in the world. The only thing was that her basic orientation was [Nadia] Boulanger. She had studied with Boulanger. She was very French oriented, very much in the Boulanger tradition, except she wasn't that kind of personality. She was a dear lady from Walla Walla; she wasn't a stern lady from France. And she was very much a...let's simply say unmarried. But she was an absolute dear. I didn't really learn much from her. She had nothing much to say except what was in her book. And if you've ever looked at the book you know it's a collection of quotations from everybody. But look, it was the only one in English.[1]

*

Ethel Peyser's tribute to Marion was published in *The Baton* of the Phi Beta Fraternity:

In Memory——Marion Bauer
November 1955

...Marion was the most disciplined person I ever knew. When exhausted after a day often starting at five in the morning and extending well into the evening, with teaching, lecturing, private music lessons, rushing through the length and breadth of New York City, she could sit down at home, dash off a few pages of copy and dictate letters without any more forcible expletive than, "Oh, I *am* tired." At the end of another such day as this she could dash from a class at The Juilliard School where she sometimes taught until 8 P. M., and hurry to the Metropolitan Opera House just in time for the opening scene, settle down in her seat, close her eyes, to listen intently. Between the acts she would talk gaily to her friends in the lobby or to those who came to her seat, and appear as proverbially fresh as the daisy...and after the performance she was always ready for a celebration. At break neck speed she drove herself, but inside she was disciplined to the point of great calm even as she sped (in spite of New York traffic tangles) to lecture, party, classroom and occasional well-loved shopping bout, with her mind and muscles marshalled without a lagging motion. Marion dwelt in a lovely haven built of her own sweet nature, the calm of which was seldom shattered.

212

She had a quick temper which she had also well leashed. Probably few realized it. But this must have been some of the motor force that blossomed in her work. She was very easily amused, loved the movies and the play, and even when troubled or very preoccupied, a good story, a bon mot or a simple joke would make her laugh. Indeed, she was a wonderful audience and a kindly critic.

In all our thirty years of friendship I never heard her speak slightingly of one person. She had a child-like nature, loved everybody and felt that everybody loved her. Therefore, many times she wasted her valued time and strength on undeserving people. This she never knew, when others deplored it, nor would she recognize it were she told!

She befriended those who sought her friendship whether they merited it or not. If she was sometimes too kindly a music critic, it was the core of her being to be kind. She lived her religion.[2]

---

[1] William Duckworth, *Talking Music: Conversations with John Cage, Philip Glass, Laurie Anderson, and Five Generations of American Experimental Composers* (New York: Schirmer Books, 1995), 62. The ellipsis is original. Brackets around [Nadia] are also original.

[2] Ethel Peyser, "In Memory––Marion Bauer," in *The Baton* of the Phi Beta Fraternity 35/1 (Nov 1955): 5 and 8. Published with Phi Beta's kind permission.

INDEX